ROYAL BLACKHEATH

Field Marshal F. Pocock

ROYAL BLACKHEATH

by Ian T. Henderson and David I. Stirk

Henderson and Stirk Ltd
Publishers

First edition 1981

Published by
Henderson and Stirk Ltd

Consultant publishers
Lund Humphries Publishers Ltd
26 Litchfield Street
London WC2

Distributed by
The Manningham Press
Drummond Road
Bradford
West Yorkshire BD8 8DH

Copies also available from
Blackheath Royal Golf Club
The Club House
Court Road
Eltham
London SE9 5AE

ISBN 0 9506549 2 2 (standard edition)
ISBN 0 9506549 3 0 (de luxe edition)

Designed by Charlton/Szyszkowski
Filmset by Keyspools Ltd,
Golborne, Lancs
Printed and bound in the
Netherlands by
Drukkerij de Lange/Van Leer BV

Acknowledgements

We are deeply grateful to the large number of people who have contributed to gathering the information on which this book is based. In the first place the Club's Historical Committee who started work as far back as 1955 under the Chairmanship of Mr N. C. Clark and who were Mr Freddie Byron, Dr James King, Mr Peter Bannister and Cmdr John Green RN Retd. Subsequently they were joined by Brigadier F. Pocock. We would like to thank the past-Captains and especially Mr Bobby Furber for his contribution to Chapter 10 (Rules of golf) and for his help in many other ways. Our research was considerably helped by Mrs Beryl Platts, Mrs Juliana Wadham, Mr James Dewar of the BBC Bristol, Mr Ralph Hyde of the Guildhall Library, and Mr J. Watson of the Local History Library, Greenwich. In Scotland we thank Mr Edward Aglen and the Honourable Company of Edinburgh Golfers, Mr George Gibb, Mr Stewart Cruden of the Bruntsfield Golf Club, Mr R. Ironside of the Royal Musselburgh Golf Club, Mr A. Rodden of the North East Fife District Library, The Signet Library, Edinburgh, Mr H. Brashaw of the Advocates' Library, Edinburgh, Sir Iain Moncreiffe of that Ilk and Mr George Draffen of Newington.

The following Golf Clubs – The President and Chairman of The Royal North Devon Golf Club, Mrs Eileen Harrison, Captain of the Blackheath Ladies' Club; Mr M. Powlesland of Caister and Great Yarmouth Golf Club, Brigadier T. G. Walker, Secretary of Royal St George's Golf Club and Mr Colin Scott of the R. & A. (for permission to examine their early minutes), Mr J. W. D. Goodban OBE, Mr J. B. Burrows, President of the Blackheath Golf Club of New South Wales, Australia (for information regarding his Club).

Our thanks are also due to our researcher Mr M. J. Gandy and to Mr Neil Rhind (for his detailed local historical knowledge), our photographer Mr Geoffrey White (who took the Blackheath photographs) and to Mrs Asa Thomas for her drawings. We wish to thank Mr John Taylor of Lund Humphries Publishers Ltd for his invaluable work as consultant publisher, Charlton/Szyszkowski for their book design and Mrs Patricia Rawson, who has seen the whole script through to its final conclusion.

Finally this book would not have been possible without the enthusiasm and devotion of Mr Donald Tindley, past-Captain and Trustee of the Royal Blackheath Golf Club. It was he who made the first contact with the authors and carried the whole project through – finding the material and photographs from the Club archives, arranging for the authors to meet Mr Geoffrey White and settle the photographic programme and subsequently arranging for Mr White to have access to the pictures and showcases at the Club. Lastly, with willing volunteers, he has organised the sale of the book by the Club.

Contents

Foreword

It is as a contribution to the social history of Great Britain, as well as the history of a Golf Club, that we at Royal Blackheath present this book.

The authors have established a remarkable fact, that the earliest golfers known by name met at Blackheath primarily as members of a secret society.

Their recorded proceedings are detailed and will be found to be very interesting, throwing as they do sidelights on the life of the times.

We who play the game are indebted to the early members of this esoteric society and their successors at Blackheath for their contribution to the development of all that goes to make up a Golf Club – clubs, balls, rules and standards of conviviality and social behaviour.

We are grateful to the authors for their painstaking research which established hitherto unsuspected facets in the history of our ancient Club.

F. Pocock
Field Marshal

Introduction

Those unfamiliar with the history of organised golf should know that it first appeared in the middle of the eighteenth century. It continued to be played at a relatively low level of activity in Scotland and at Blackheath and Manchester (1819) in England, until the middle of the nineteenth century. The arrival of the cheap gutta golf ball in 1848 provided the first impetus for the growth of the game. Thereafter a number of factors–the Industrial Revolution leading to the growth of early easy railway communications, seaside resorts and holidays–provided opportunities for all kinds of sporting activities such as cricket, soccer, rugger and golf. This culminated in the great worldwide 'craze' for golf in the last quarter of the nineteenth century.

Blackheath Golf Club has been known wherever golf is played for its legendary date of having been 'instituted in 1608'. This legend has been in existence for nearly 200 years. Our first task, aided by the considerable research work done by the Club's Historical Committee, has been to search once more for some explanation of how this date was arrived at. We have been able to chronicle the arrival of golf at Blackheath and to explain in more detail how James I brought the game with him when his Court arrived in London in 1603.

Our examination of the Blackheath records has, however, revealed an entirely new explanation as to how organised golf was started, both in Scotland and at Blackheath. The feature of all early organised golfing societies was their commitment to dining and conviviality. This can be understood now that we know that it was groups of freemasons who had the happy idea of adding golf as a healthy form of exercise prior to their dining. With this explanation we are able at least to speculate how the tradition of 1608 came into being and how it is confirmed by evidence going back to 1766.

Blackheath was, in fact, to play a unique role in the expansion of the game of golf outside Scotland. It was not unlike a plant, almost dormant for 250 years, which suddenly decides to flower and then dies, spreading its seeds far and wide. The course of seven holes was inland in character and was inevitably doomed to be overrun and eventually abandoned. A similar fate overtook Bruntsfield, Leith and Musselburgh in Scotland. It was not long after the gutta ball arrived in 1848 that the first great Foursomes Tournament took place at St Andrews in 1857 and was won by Blackhealth. This gave the Club considerable prestige. In 1864, with the active help of the members of Blackheath, the Club at Westward Ho! was founded and Blackheath members went forth and supported the formation of Clubs such as Royal Wimbledon, Royal Liverpool (Hoylake), Royal St George's (Sandwich) and Great Yarmouth. The same encouragement was given overseas to Bombay and Calcutta. Those prominent members of the Club whose missionary zeal resulted in the formation of some of the greatest courses in England have certainly left behind worthy monuments to their enthusiasm.

Happily, when golf ended on the Heath, the Club was able to amalgamate with the Eltham Club which occupied a magnificent period Clubhouse. Here, too, rooms have been set aside as a small museum. Apart from the Royal & Ancient, it is the only Club in the country to have one and it is supported by the Historical Committee. Among its many possessions–portraits and trophies–the most outstanding must surely be its collection of eighteenth- and nineteenth-century clubs, particularly the irons. To be able to inspect the portrait of Henry Callender (1807) and see the actual putter which appears in it, gives an authenticity to the Collection which must be unique.

We hope that this book will make a fresh contribution to the history of golf and at the same time encourage the Club members to understand what lies behind the traditions that they have inherited.

Chapter 1 The arrival of golf at Blackheath

Long before golf had become a universal sport, it was referred to as the 'Royal and Ancient' game. So much so that when the Society of St Andrews Golfers sought the Royal patronage of William IV in 1834, the title they submitted was 'The Royal and Ancient Golf Club of St Andrews', and the ultimate change of title conferred 'Royal' status on St Andrews. The significance of the phrase 'Royal and Ancient' was that it implied that it had been the sport of kings, and it was the Stuart dynasty, first in Scotland and later in England, which has always been associated with the origins of golf in this country. Thereafter no British monarch took any interest until modern times.

The early Stuart Kings of Scotland had necessarily to concern themselves with the defence of their kingdom. In order to encourage their subjects to keep themselves in training for war, they had to make sure that their leisure hours were not diverted by sporting activities. They did this by passing Acts of Parliament forbidding the playing of football, etc. In 1457, for the first time, (James II Parl. 14, Cap. 64) 'gouff' was included in the ban and the stricture was repeated in two subsequent reigns (James III 1470 Parl. 6, Cap. 44 and James IV 1491 Parl. 3, Cap. 32). In 1501 the Treaty of Glasgow was entered into between James IV of Scotland and Henry VII of England and a truce between the two countries was achieved. This was cemented by the betrothal of Henry's daughter Margaret Tudor, then aged nine, to James IV and she duly married him at the age of 16. It was the descendant of this marriage who ultimately unified the Crowns of England and Scotland in 1603.

As a result of the peace, James IV conceded that there was no need to continue his ban on golf and we find from the accounts of the Lord High Treasurer of Scotland between 1502–03 that there are several entries for the purchase of golf clubs and balls for the King at St Johnstoun, Perth.

In 1567 James IV's granddaughter Mary Queen of Scots was charged with unseemly conduct for playing golf and pall mall at Seton House, East Lothian, a few days after the murder of her husband Lord Darnley (*Inventories of Mary Queen of Scots*, Preface p.lxx–1563). Her recently-born son was to become James VI of Scotland and when it became obvious that Queen Elizabeth I of England would never marry, he was recognised as being heir presumptive to the throne of England. Long before James came to the throne, Lord Cecil, Elizabeth's Secretary of State, was sending emissaries to Scotland to instruct the future king in the ways of the English Court. They stayed as guests of Sir

Portrait of James I by de Critz (by permission of the National Gallery of Scotland)

Henry Prince of Wales by Isaac Oliver

John Seton at Seton House, mentioned above, where James VI was also a frequent visitor. Sir John Seton also spent some time at Queen Elizabeth's Court. In 1603 Elizabeth died and the Scottish Court proceeded to London. Besides the Palace of Whitehall there were then three palaces near London which were occupied from time to time by the Court–Hampton Court (on the Thames near Kingston, Surrey), Nonsuch (built by Henry VIII between Ewell and Sutton in Surrey but which never survived the Civil War in the seventeenth century and was ultimately demolished) and finally Greenwich (five miles down the river from the City of London). In the area adjacent to these palaces it would have been possible for the members of the Court to play golf, and we are lucky enough to have documentary evidence that they did play, and of one royal player in particular–Henry Frederick, Prince of Wales, son of James I. Here is a picture of him as a young man.

Henry was born in February 1594 at Stirling Castle and was growing into an outstanding young man and the hope for the future of the nation, when he died tragically at the age of 17. His short life has been much written about and from the number of portraits of him that have survived, it is clear that he was the object of much admiration. He was a lively character, much given also to athletic pursuits. The French Ambassador, Monsieur de Borderie, in a letter to his friend Monsieur de Puisieux dated 31 October 1606 says: 'He plays willingly enough at tennis and at another Scots diversion very like Mall; but this always with persons older than himself, as if he despised those of his own age.' (Drake's edition of Hasted, *History of Kent*, 'Hundred of Blackheath,' p. 120).

There is the further reference: 'for when the prince was playing at goff, and having warned his tutor who was standing by in conversation that he was going to strike the ball, and having lifted up the goff-club, some one observing "Beware, sir, that you hit not Mr Newton!"' (his tutor) (Isaac d'Israeli's *Curiosities of Literature*, p. 247) and also *Life of Henry Prince of Wales*, (Birch 1760). This typically human incident is a unique reference to golf at that time and indeed for many years thereafter and may bring with it the confirmation we need that he would have played the game at or near Blackheath. Charlton House, Blackheath, was built for Prince Henry, and one of his two tutors Mr (later Sir) Adam Newton, occupied Charlton Lodge, later moving into Charlton House (which still stands today) when Prince Henry died. When the Court were in residence at Greenwich and were seeking suitable ground on which to play golf, they climbed to the high ground above the palace and found what space they wanted.

It should be remembered that the Scottish members of the Court arrived in much larger numbers than anyone has yet appreciated. On pp. 147–51* we give the names of fifty of them who came South with James I and each of them came with a large retinue of servants and household officers, so the number must have run into several thousands. It was from these nobility and their followers that the golfers would have come.

In 1604 William Mayne was appointed Royal Clubmaker but it has proved impossible to find out anything about him. Some few years later in 1618 James I had developed the sale of monopolies as a means of raising money. One Melville together with Berwick, an associate, thought it worthwhile to obtain a monopoly on the sale of golf balls and they obtained an instrument to this effect on 4 August 1618 at Salisbury, Wiltshire in England. They themselves were not ballmakers (Melville was in fact Quartermaster to Moreton Horse, an irregular unit of unsavoury reputation run by Lord Moreton) and the main supply undoubtedly was imported from Holland which had a feather ballmaking centre at Goirle, near Tilburg. The balls were used both for tennis and golf. In 1631 Melville came unstuck trying to enforce his monopoly in Edinburgh against one Dickson, seizing not only balls but a set of clubs made for the King. It was found that the monopoly had never been confirmed. This episode serves to indicate that golf was an active game at that time; and the order that Dickson had made for the King further confirms that Charles I did play golf. However, although it is possible to confirm that Charles I and James II (when he was Duke of York

* List of Scottish Courtiers compiled by Mrs Beryl Platts (author of *Origins of Heraldry* Procter Press 1980)

in Edinburgh) did play the game, there is no documentary evidence that they played when in London. Furthermore, considerable research has failed to produce evidence that golf was played in London during the seventeenth century other than the request for a bye-law to protect passers-by from golfers in Tothill Fields, Westminster, in 1658, and such players would almost certainly have been Scots. These, therefore, are the circumstances which first brought golf to Blackheath.

Although the Crowns of Scotland and England were now held by James, the two countries were not to be united for another hundred years. There were definite advantages for the Scots, apart from the many favours to Scottish members of James's Court. This is hardly surprising seeing that the King was brought up in Scotland as a Scot, and would appreciate the companionship of his fellow countrymen when he came down to London. The old hatred between England and Scotland was still strong, although it had become less vehement. Englishmen knew little of Scotland and James's generosity to Scottish favourites caused them to be intensely unpopular. Trade was being opened up between the two countries and in 1607 Parliament ruled that the Scots were not to be debarred from the Merchants' Societies. Sir Christopher Piggot immediately made an attack in Parliament on the Scots (13 February 1607) and Sir John Ramsey of the King's Bedchamber complained to the King on behalf of his fellow countrymen and the King had to send for Lord Salisbury. This incident is quoted as the background which accounted for the London merchants' fear that they were about to suffer competition from the Scots. Fierce debates in Parliament on the question of free trade with Scotland and naturalisation of the Scots resident in England followed, but in the end free trade with England and the Colonies was granted to the Scots. Merchants came south and ultimately prospered in the City of London and in building the Empire. Nevertheless, the result was a long history of understandable hostility which meant that the Scots must have tended to keep their own company in London. For example, when the coffee houses started to be popular in London towards the end of the seventeenth century, the Scots were known to frequent particular houses.

We have to wait until the Silver Club dated 1766 for the first evidence that golf was being played on the Heath. It was followed by a notice in the press in 1785 headed 'The GOFF CLUB', Assembly House, Blackheath. The original Chocolate House was opened in 1702 and was built to serve the needs of what was beginning to become a residential suburb of London within easy reach of the city by coach. The Club was adjacent to the Heath, on what is now West Green, but around 1787 its Assembly Rooms were transferred to the Green Man or Bowling Green House opposite. This had an even older history having originally been called the Bowling Green, which term appears in the Parliamentary Survey of 1649. In Evelyn's *Diary*, 1 May 1683, he mentions a new tavern at the Bowling Green, subsequently called the Green Man Hotel, rebuilt in 1869 and finally demolished in 1974.

Here are two maps, one taken from Camden's *Britannica* (1694 edition) which shows that Blackheath at that time was not even a village. The second map, dated 1746, shows the size of the Heath together with the urban development that had taken place in the intervening years. The course, adjacent to the walled-in grounds of Greenwich Palace, was at the west end of the Heath and the Chocolate House and the Green Man were the most convenient headquarters available to golfers travelling down from the City of London for the day. In the seventeenth century the Heath became one of the chief sources for excavating gravel for the building of London–particularly after the Great Fire of London in 1666. Eventually in 1843 the 'worked out' gravel pits became the hazards for the redesigned golf course–which became known as the Hazard Course. The number of holes was increased from 5 to 7, and, during its existence it never had any bunkers in the form we know today. With the end of golf on the Heath after World War I, and the subsequent dumping of rubble from the Blitz in World War II, the old gravel pits have been filled in and there now remains only a trace of the demands made on the Heath to build so much of London or of its historic link with golf.

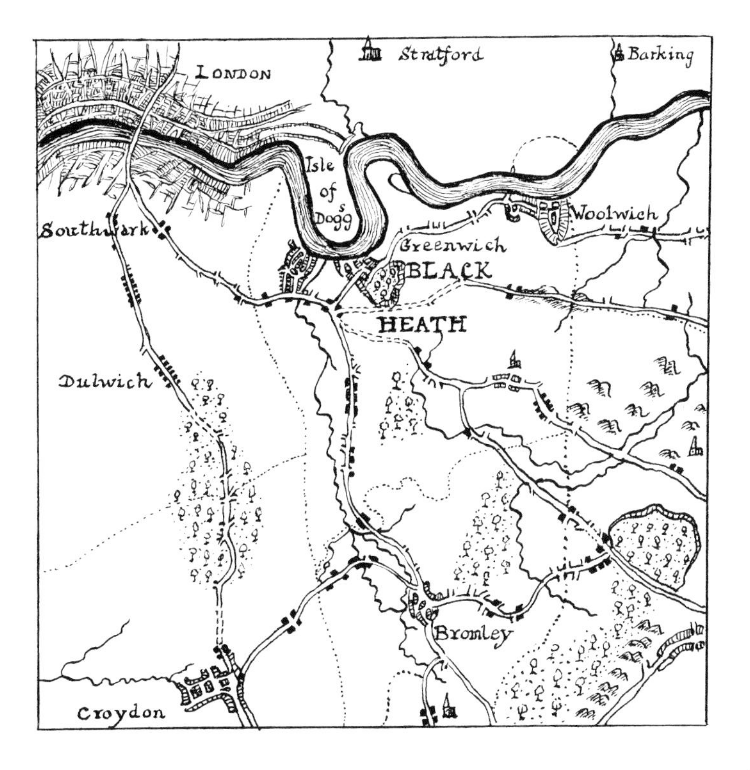

Extract of map from Camden's *Britannica*, 1694 edition, showing the Blackheath area

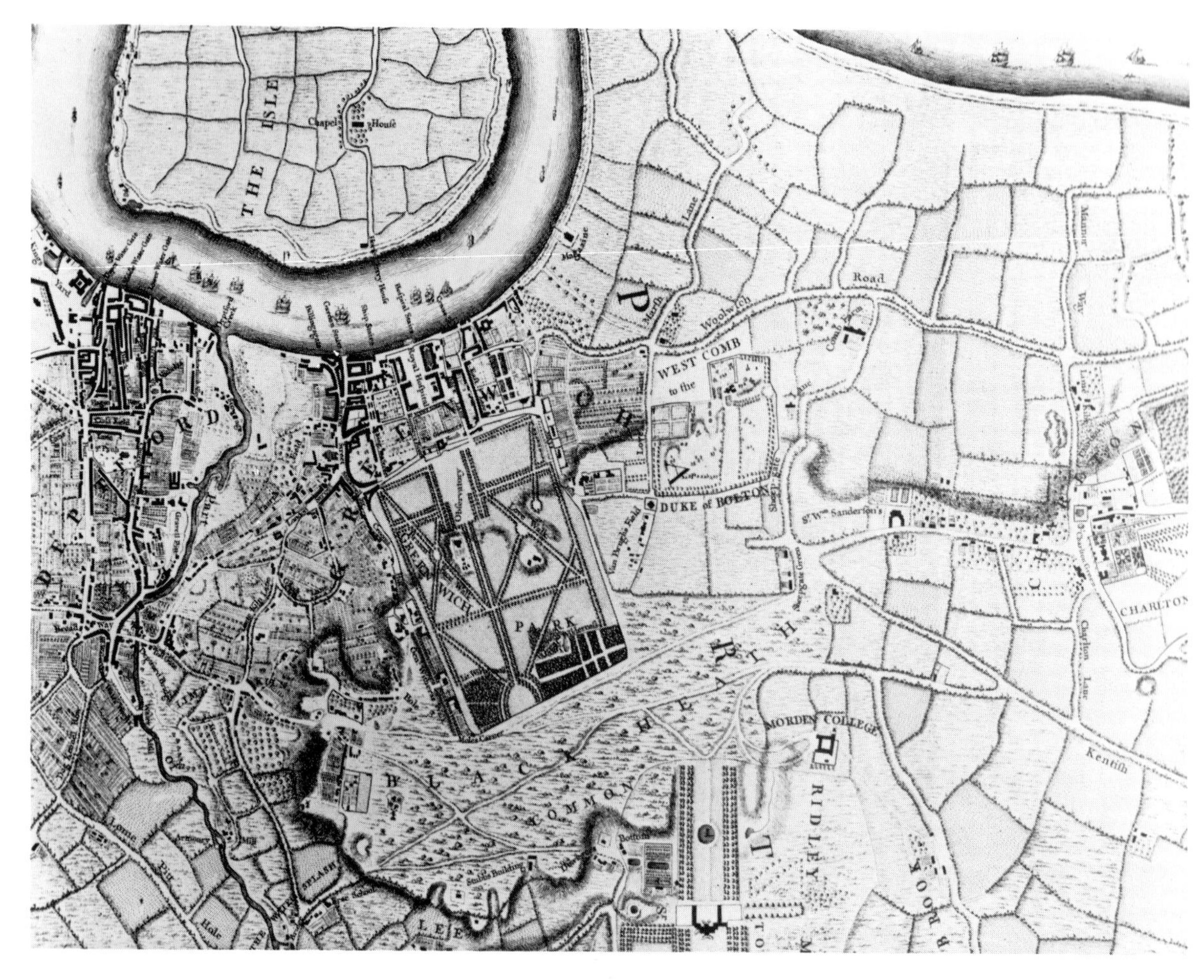

'An exact survey of the City's of London, Westminster, ye Borough of Southwark and the country near ten miles round' by John Rocque, 1746.

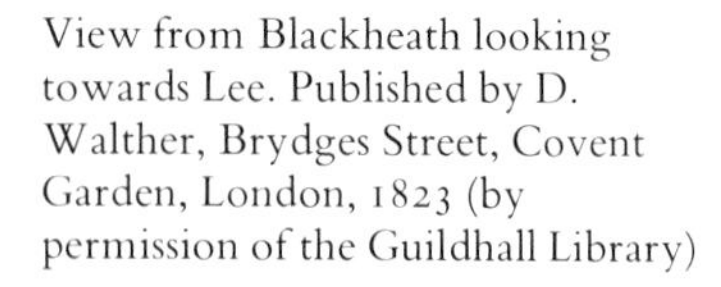

View from Blackheath looking towards Lee. Published by D. Walther, Brydges Street, Covent Garden, London, 1823 (by permission of the Guildhall Library)

Chapter 2 The organisation by Scottish Freemasons of the early Golfing Societies

Having seen how golf arrived at Blackheath at the beginning of the seventeenth century, we now come to the problem of how and when the first Golfing Societies were formed and whether any fresh light can be thrown on how the Blackheath Club acquired the tradition of 'instituted 1608'.

As far back as 1808, the *Edinburgh Almanack* listed the leading Golfing Societies and when they claimed to have been formed, and thereafter there has been considerable argument and discussion on the subject. One writer, Robert Browning in *A History of Golf* (Dent 1955), advanced the theory that it was the advent of competition for a prize that resulted in what is now called 'incorporation', or the forming of a Club or Society. Thus when the Gentlemen Golfers of Edinburgh (later the Honourable Company of Edinburgh Golfers) succeeded in getting the City of Edinburgh to put up a Silver Club for 'open' competition in 1744, they were requested to draw up the first Rules of Golf which governed the way in which the game was to be played, because there was a prize at stake. While this may account for the necessity for establishing rules for playing the game, it did not explain how they achieved exclusivity, and there is no evidence that a Society, or Club, was formed solely as a result of acquiring a prize for which to play.

Other writers delved into the surviving minutes and looked for documentary evidence, with the result that the six Societies with their generally accepted dates of foundation are as follows (under their present titles):

The Royal Burgess Golfing Society of Edinburgh (instituted 1735 but no evidence until 1770)
The Honourable Company of Edinburgh Golfers (founded 1744 but first regulations for Club 1764)
The Royal and Ancient Golf Club of St Andrews (the R. & A.) (founded 1754)
The Bruntsfield Golf Club (founded 1761 but no evidence until 1787)
The Royal Musselburgh Golf Club (founded 1774 but no evidence until 1784)
The Royal Blackheath Golf Club ('instituted' 1608 but no evidence until 1766)

In establishing the above table, everyone has so far assumed that the primary object of the formation of a Society was just to play golf, but the re-examination of the Blackheath minutes produced evidence that caused us to look at the early histories of all these Societies from an entirely different angle, which has revealed a logical explanation for what transpired at that time. Golf was not the primary objective and it was groups of Scottish freemasons who adopted it as a healthy form of exercise prior to their feasting and were thus responsible for the earliest form of organised golf. The systematic destruction of early minutes has successfully concealed this fact for well over two hundred years but, by looking at the recorded activity of those six early Golfing Societies, we can show how this explanation is justified.

Royal Blackheath Golf Club

The membership of the Club was predominantly Scottish and it possesses a Silver Club dating from 1766 and silver balls attached to it with the names of the Captains inscribed on them from that date. The minutes of the Club prior to 1800 are missing but the account books from 1787 survive as do the minutes of a separate Winter Club formed in 1789, called the Knuckle Club. Parts of this latter Club's minutes were excised but from those minutes remaining we learn that it had initiation ceremonies, insignia and its own Anniversary Dinner celebrating its foundation on 17 January 1789, and not the institution date of 1608. Its members were referred to as 'Brother' or 'Knuckle' and it was incorporated as a masonic lodge. When it dissolved in 1825 its members decided in future 'to meet only as golfers'.

The minutes prior to 1800 were alleged to have been destroyed (in *Chronicles of Blackheath Golfers* (W. E. Hughes 1897)) in a disastrous fire, but as subsequently explained, it is clear that there was no fire and that they must have been deliberately destroyed. The Captain in 1766, Alexander Duncan, a master mason, provides a most interesting link with the Company of Edinburgh Golfers and the R. & A. and it is not surprising therefore to find that its customs were similar to those of the other Scottish Societies. The members wore uniform, had regular dinners, were fined sometimes for non-attendance, had to pay up for the birth of a child or on marriage and had separate bets books, toasts, etc. To this day Blackheath Golf Club celebrates its Anniversary with a degree of ceremony which is unmatched by any Golf Club, and, moreover, has been doing so at least since 1785.

The Honourable Company of Edinburgh Golfers

The Edinburgh City Council gave a Silver Club for open competition in 1744 but it was not until 1764 that the Club's membership regulations were drawn up and the Club managed to get the competition for the Silver Club confined to its own membership. It was then decided to build a 'Golfing House' which was designed as a tavern; this was let to a tenant and the Society reserved accommodation in it. A minute of 2 July 1768 reads as follows:

A sketch of William St Clair of Roslin after the portrait by Sir George Chalmers

William St Clair of Roslin (who was Captain of the Company in 1761, 66, 70 and 71) was not only an outstanding golfer but an excellent archer and a member of the Company of Royal Archers. His place in masonry was outstanding; in 1736 the Grand Lodge of Scotland was formed and he was elected the Grand Master, following a claim (which he had then renounced) that his family had been hereditary Grandmasters of Scotland for 200 years. He was also Captain of the R. & A. in 1764, 66 and 68 – winning the Silver Club and holing the 22 holes in 1764 in the remarkable score of 121

'This day William St. Clair of Roslin Esquire, the Undoubted representative of the honourable and heritable G.M.M. of SCOTLAND In the presence of Alexander Keith Esquire Captain of the honourable Company of Golfers and other worthy members of the Golfing Company, all Masons, the G: (sic) now in his GRAND CLIMAX of Golfing laid the foundation stone of the Golfing House in the S.E. Corner thereof by THREE STROKES with the MALLETT

Alexr Peacocke M.M.

Alexr Keith Capt.
Wm. ST: Clair G.M.M.
Robert Henderson
Alexr Duncan M.M.
Capt Blackheath &
Old Capt of St. Andrews
James Cheape
William Hogart
Alexr Orme M.M.
Robert Beatson M.M.
Henry Bethune G.M.
Richard Tod Sub. G.M.
Henry Seton 2 Capt. M.M.
Ben Gordon'

The most striking thing about this minute is that it states that all members present were masons and gives their names and masonic rank. It was the Grandmaster Mason of Scotland who laid the foundation stone, and not the Captain of the Club. Furthermore at that time Alexander MacDougall was Secretary of the Club and also of the Grand Lodge of Scotland (1755–1774). Note also the presence of Alexander Duncan, M.M., the Captain of Blackheath in 1766, Captain of the R. & A. in 1756, 61 and 81 and Captain of the Edinburgh Company in 1771.

The Company was organised on very similar lines to Blackheath at that time and both had golf courses of 5 holes. The requirement was not only to play golf but dine afterwards and there were uniforms and bets recorded in the bets books and fines on certain occasions. The election of new members was closely controlled and the 'black ball' was used.

In the 1780s the Company prospered financially but from 1800 onwards a steady decline set in, mainly through members failing to pay their subscriptions and failing to turn up for the dinners which had been ordered. By the 1820s they were raising money on mortgage of their Golfing House and the failure to pay the interest on this finally resulted in the public auction of the clubroom contents in 1832 for £106, the Golfing House being sold in 1834. The Club was revived in 1836 by which time it had left Leith and moved to Musselburgh. The Company's minutes are missing from 1745–47 (following the '45 Rebellion and the Battle of Culloden) and again from 1796–1825; sparse between 1825–31 and there are no records at all between 1831–36.

There can be no question that this Company in its early years was run by the freemasons without necessarily being a lodge in the formal sense, but it had no proper constitution for the election of a Captain and governing body. The financial disaster which beset the Club which boasted the leading citizens of Edinburgh must be attributed perhaps to waning masonic interest. If there had been harmony in the Society it is inconceivable that the Club's paintings and belongings should have been sold up for such a paltry sum. Resuscitated in 1836 at Musselburgh, it prospered thereafter and eventually moved to Gullane, East Lothian and created Muirfield, one of the finest golf courses in the world.

The Edinburgh Burgess Club

The Club minutes start in 1770 and in 1773 record that three members of the Society of Golfers admit Hart and 14 others as members at a subscription of 2s 6d. The Club claimed to have been in existence long before this and, in fact, 1735 is claimed as the date of the start of the Society, but there are no minutes in existence to prove this. This Club had a uniform of scarlet jackets etc. 'as done by other societies of golfers'. In 1806 there was a bitter row between two factions which nearly caused the demise of the Society but it was eventually revived in 1808. The Chronicles of the Royal Burgess give the reason for the dispute as originating in an interpretation of the 'stymie' rule in what was to be their competition for a golf medal but the minutes covering that period in their history were destroyed.

The Chronicles also devote a whole chapter (pp.61–72) to social life, which is the story of the dinners (with similar requirements to those recorded in the other Societies) and of how the dinners gradually died out, but as late as 1838 the masonic 'three times three' toast was still drunk. The Annual Meeting was always celebrated and members specifically required to attend.

The Bruntsfield Golf Club

Robert Clark in his *Golf a Royal and Ancient Game* (1875) stated that this Society claims 1761 for its original formation, but had no original list of members and the first minute book dates from 1787: 'Present Alexander Brown and 9 others when it changes its name from Society into Club'. In 1790 there is a minute saying that the Club has been in existence for thirty years. They had an 'anniversary day' (see minute dated June 1788). They used uniform and celebrated their centenary at the Freemasons' Hall, Edinburgh, in 1861. At the Dinner the Captain, quoting from the minutes, said that there was evidence that the Bruntsfield Society broke away from the Burgess Club at Bruntsfield owing to strong feeling regarding the loyal toast. George Lorimer, joint author of *Reminiscences of the Old Bruntsfield Links*, written in 1902, said he could not find evidence of this in the minutes but, subsequently, lost all his notes and some of the minutes. Nevertheless this story has a ring of truth about it, because there must have been Jacobite sympathies in many a Society at that time. On 3 October 1801 there is a minute recording an order for '1 dozen caps and aprons . . . expense to be paid out of the Admission Fund'. They could hardly be required for golf, nor for staff and must have been required for masonic admissions.

Royal Musselburgh Golf Club

According again to Robert Clark, this Club claims 1774 as the date of formation but the minutes of the first ten years are missing. The minutes do not start until 1784 but the period from 1774 is covered by the names attached to the medals 'of the quaint old cup'. There is evidence of a bets book but no mention of uniform. In 1798 government became the object of their charity and they gave 'Their myte to the voluntary subscription in aid of the government–5gns'!

The Royal and Ancient Golf Club of St Andrews

Unlike other Golfing Societies who have minutes 'missing,' minutes are in existence from 1754 when the Silver Club was subscribed for and Rules of Golf adopted together with a most complicated method of finding the 'Captain of the Golf' laid down. It was a competition 'open' to anyone and was advertised in the press. As a competition it aroused no great enthusiasm–the first event attracted only four competitors, and in 1757 and 1760 no-one entered for it at all.

The minutes from 1754–1766 contain no information relating to social activities, but on 4 May 1766 an additional minute book, termed the 'Book of Record' (and running concurrently with Minute Book No. 1) appears, containing the first details of social activities. The following resolution then appears:

'Wee (sic) the Nobleman and Gentlemen Subscribing Admirers of the Ancient and very healthfull Exercise of the Golf, and at the same time having the Interest and prosperity of the Ancient City of St. Andrews the alma mater of the Golf at heart. DID this day aggree To meet once every fortnight by Eleven of the Clock at the Golf House and to play around of the Links (in terms of the Regulations of the Silver Club). To dine together at Baillie Glass's and to pay each a shilling for his dinner. The absent as well as the present. This obligation to be binding upon each of the subscribers, during the six months following this date and for every Summer hereafter Unless the Subscribers shall give in a Diclinature to be Sustained and

Recorded in this Book. The Captain and his Councill Finding that the Members of the Club had Signed upon detached pieces of paper Did and hereby do Authorize and appoint their Clerk to affix their Names as obligatory upon their persons to fullfill the promises'
(*The Story of the R. & A.*, J. R. Salmond, 1956, p.43)

Here we learn for the first time of the formation of a Club governed by the 'Captain and his Council' and the obligation to dine once a fortnight. In 1770 the term Society of Golfers is first used. There is no mention of uniform, but they obviously had one as there was a minute in 1780 stating that uniforms were in bad condition. There may also have been bets books, although they do not appear until 1815. The sparseness of the early minutes makes us wonder whether there was not an earlier record book containing details of social activities: Seeing that Alexander Duncan, M.M., was Captain in 1756 and 1761 and William St Clair of Roslin, G.M.M. of Scotland in 1764, 66 and 68 it is unlikely that there were no social activities.

Dr James Grierson in his *History of St Andrews* (first edition 1801), stated that although the Silver Club was apparently played for every year yet the dignity of the 'Captain of the Company' was really elective and that it was 'always fixed before proceeding to the field who is to return victorious for this honour'. This statement was probably true and the problem was later solved by the Captain Elect being the sole competitor for the Silver Club and winning it by driving himself into office at the Autumn Meeting. This was also the occasion for holding the Annual Dinner for which we have a description by Dr T. F. Dibdin in 1836, in his *A Bibliographical Antiquarian and Picturesque tour in the Northern Counties of England and in Scotland*, vol. 2, pp.87f.

'After dinner the mysteries were entered upon. The silver baton, staff or club (there was only one in those days) which is used to propel the ball onwards, was placed on the table before the President; having silver balls . . . fastened to the body of the baton. Then came a shorter silver club, called a putter, also encircled by silver balls. The candidate, on his admission to the Golfing Club by ballot, comes forward to the side of the President, who, raising the putter aloft, the former courteously receives it, and kisses one or more of the balls.'

In 1853 the Committee requested Mr John Whyte-Melville to lay the foundation stone of the new Clubhouse with masonic honours (see Everard, *History of the Royal and Ancient Golf Club*, p.156), but according to J. R. Salmond, *The Story of the R. & A.*, p.86, Major Belshes laid the foundation stone on Whitsunday

1854 'with full masonic honours'.

These brief histories of the Golfing Societies have similar characteristics, the most important of which was the obligation to dine after playing golf. They had Club uniforms, ceremonies, fines in the form of drink for absence or other offences, toasts, including the masonic 'three times three'. New membership was controlled with the use of a 'black ball', when necessary. Attendance at dinners and the guests were recorded and often details of the meal. There was never a great deal in those days to mention about golf except the bets on matches which were usually entered in a separate book and were by no means all related to golf matches. An officer called the Registrar also frequently appears.

The way in which these Societies were organised on similar lines could have been no accident, and once the Grand Master Mason of Scotland and his fellow freemasons had been observed laying the foundation stone of a new Golfing House at Leith in 1767, there can hardly be any doubt that the attractive concept of playing golf before banqueting was organised by them. Golf historians up to now have never been able to explain why there was this obligation to dine after playing golf; nor have they looked at the activities of the early Societies as a whole. We believe that the explanations now offered permit the early history of these Societies to be examined on a far more logical basis than ever before.

Freemasons shared a secret and, as time went on, they played golf with non-masons, who were not admitted to their ceremonies, or mysteries as they were referred to. It will have been noticed that the Burgess, Bruntsfield, Musselburgh and Blackheath Societies all have foundation dates earlier than their first minutes and that considerable parts of the Edinburgh Company's minutes are missing. We believe that the explanation for these missing minutes lies in the admission of non-masons to the Societies, owing to the decline in the number of golfers who were masons. Once this process reached a certain stage, the Society decided to destroy any evidence which might reveal their secrets. In so doing, they were remarkably successful in covering their tracks for so many years, and this was done in accordance with masonic practice.

The Dutch had been playing golf as early as 1297 and by the sixteenth and seventeenth centuries it had become a national pastime. Thanks to the researches of Steven van Hengel (*Early Golf* 1972) we now know that it was actively played in some 29 Dutch cities. There are examples in existence of the clubs and balls they used and their golfing activities are recorded on ice and on land in large numbers of beautiful Dutch and Flemish landscape pictures. For no obvious reason the game was to die out completely early in the first half of the eighteenth century: it was replaced for a time by Het Kolven or mini (indoor) golf–if it could be called golf at all. The game of Pall Mall (after which Pall Mall in London is named) with a stroke so similar to golf, was also to disappear and likewise to become miniaturised and appear as crocquet. There was clear evidence that there was a decline in 'manly' sporting activity on the Continent at this period.

On the other hand golf in Scotland up to the middle of the nineteenth century could not be described by any stretch of the imagination as a national game and did not reach the West Coast of Scotland until the mid nineteenth century. We have some indication of the membership of those six early clubs (1750–1850) and judging from their minutes their maximum combined strength at any time was some 500 playing members. Here is a record of the growth in the number of Societies;

1800	7	1870	34
1850	17	1880	60
1860	25		

The membership for all that was pitifully small and even by 1881 only totalled around 5,000, of which by then three English Clubs accounted for 1136. There were admittedly a number of local communities on the East Coast of Scotland who played golf but it must always be remembered that it was a rich man's game and the numbers involved could only have been small. This is confirmed by the lack of illustrations and pictures and indeed written comment about the game. The first and only golfing scene in the eithteenth century so far discovered is the watercolour of Bruntsfield Links by Paul Sandby RA painted in 1747. We know of no other eighteenth-century landscape. There were a few well-known portraits but, although the sitters appeared with a golf club and in uniform, these were instigated by their fellow masons as a mark of their respect for those who were well known socially to each other. This came about as a result of the masonic dining custom.

Although golf was an ideal form of exercise for freemasons who were to dine after playing, we must wonder what appeal golf had to other citizens and why it did not attract more support. The great deterrent was expense but the game may not have had quite the attraction of today's game. The ball was relatively satisfactory but, with a set of wooden clubs together with one iron club for getting out of difficult places, it inspired no technical improvements until the arrival of the gutta ball in 1848. In the next 40 years both clubs and balls were transformed and the technique of the game began to evolve and fascinate the player.

If the game had not been organised by the freemasons it would probably only have survived as a quaint Scottish pastime and would never have been developed into the game it is today–the debt we owe to the freemasons is considerable.

The eighteenth century saw the growing popularity of coffee houses–followed by social clubs and all kinds of societies, and indeed Speculative Masonry–all were part of a general social pattern. Many people will be curious about the early history of freemasonry and the circumstances in which the freemasons first organised themselves and then introduced organised golf. In the Middle Ages operative masonry came into being, centred round the builders of our cathedrals. They had operative trade secrets and used the Masonic Word. This period was followed by what has been termed the metamorphosis of the Masonic Secret when 'gentlemen' or 'accepted' masons appeared. By the beginning of the eighteenth century the Masonic Secret acquired a 'new look' and became what was known as Speculative Masonry, which maintained the link with the art of building and the traditions which went with it. For our part we are looking at a period in Scottish history when, at the beginning of the eighteenth century, Speculative Masonry was growing. Yet there were divided loyalties amongst Scotsmen–to the 'king in exile' and his Jacobite followers and to the Hanoverian Crown of Britain. Catholics had not yet been forbidden to become masons and there were Jacobite lodges, but with the Scottish Rebellions of 1715 and 1745, secret societies were undoubtedly under considerable suspicion. Having survived this difficult period, the turn of the nineteenth century saw declining masonic influence and this perhaps explains the decline in the popularity of organised golf in the 1820s and 1830s. The dining commitment was on its way out and in the future Golf Clubs were founded whose object was to provide opportunity to play golf.

Anthony Sampson writing about Clubs in general in his book *Anatomy of Britain* (Hodder & Stoughton 1962) sums up most aptly what happened:

> 'The point of a club is not who it lets in, but who it keeps out. The club is based on two ancient British ideas–the segregation of classes, and the segregation of sexes: and they remain insistent on keeping people out, long after they have stopped wanting to come in . . . .'

Nevertheless, some of the original Societies have been left with a strong sense of tradition, of the origins of which present members are unlikely to be aware. This explains why the majority of the original Societies still have no lady membership. All that we can say with certainty is that these early Societies had similar customs not related to golf, they shared a secret–again not related to golf–and that they were not formed with the primary object of playing golf. What was originally offered was in today's terminology a 'package deal'–golf, dinner and the mysteries.

Those who took up this offer had to be well-to-do, and from what we know of the membership of those early Societies, they attracted the leading members of the community–nobles, gentlemen, advocates, bankers, flourishing tradesmen and the like. Furthermore, in those days freemasons were often to be seen in public, in ceremonial processions, wearing uniform and regalia. But the requirement for golfers to wear uniform on the green and at their dinners, had at that time nothing to do with the later regulation to wear a red jacket on public courses, as a warning to passers by.

We may conclude by saluting those groups of masons who started and maintained organised golf for the first hundred years of its existence. As we have already observed, they succeeded in keeping the game alive when it might so easily have suffered the same fate as golf in Holland and disappeared. Dining and conviviality belonged to that age and golf was a most useful associate; simple and straightforward to play, 'the very healthfull Exercise of the Golf' as they called it.

Mezzotint of William Innes, taken from a portrait by L. F. Abbott RA 1790 and engraved by Valentine Green. The plate was dedicated to the Society of Golfers at Blackheath

Henry Callender by L. F. Abbott RA 1807. In the possession of the Club

Old Alick, Portrait of Alick Brotherston, caddy and holecutter, by R. S. E. Gallen of the Greenwich School 1839. In the possession of the Club

'Golf at Blackheath', 1875, by F. P. Hopkins
(see Key on p. 67)

W. F. Dyer and present and past-
Captains at a Captains' Dinner

Anniversary Dinner Ceremony
(see Chapter 11)

Corporal Sharpe. A watercolour signed 'C. E. Cundell', apparently dated 1839 but believed to be 1833 (see p. 45). Recently discovered at the Club

Chapter 3 Blackheath prior to 1843

The Blackheath records go back just under two hundred years and tell us a great deal about the first organised Club outside Scotland. Their history divides itself into three eras–the first from their 'institution' to the end of that extraordinary fifty-year period when they had two separate Clubs–the Blackheath Golf Club or Summer Club and the Knuckle Club, later to become the Winter Club, with which we shall now deal.

Chronicles of Blackheath Golfers by W. E. Hughes (one time Captain and then Secretary of the Club), published privately by Chapman & Hall 1897, commented on and edited the minutes as he found them, without endeavouring to investigate how 'instituted 1608' appeared. Since he wrote the *Chronicles*, two World Wars have intervened but the archives and treasures are still intact. The documents and relics which have survived are as follows:

1 *A Silver Club with silver balls* and the names of captains on them presented in 1766 by Mr Henry Foot of whom no trace has yet been found.

The Silver Club dated 1766, presented by Henry Foot, with the silver balls attached

2 *The accounts of the Blackheath Club* starting from 1787, and the *Bets Book of the Club* starting from 1800. Surviving relics include the magnificent collection of antique golf clubs and feathery balls (see p. 124), two punch bowls, two claret jugs or jorams and two ivory gavels. They also possessed at that time a valuable tent which was erected on the Heath, was bought in 1792 for £38.5.6. and used for many years thereafter.

One of the two punch bowls belonging to the Club

Enlargement of the decoration on the punch bowl

The jorams belonging to the Blackheath Golf Club and to the Knuckle Club (one of each pair being marked 'Treasurer's Jug') together with the punch bowls of the Club

The gavels belonging to the Blackheath Golf Club and the Knuckle Club

3 *The minutes of the Knuckle Club* less the first four pages, starting in 1787 and are accompanied by an account book. Surviving relics are two ivory gavels, two one-gallon jorams and the Knuckle Club Gold Medal.

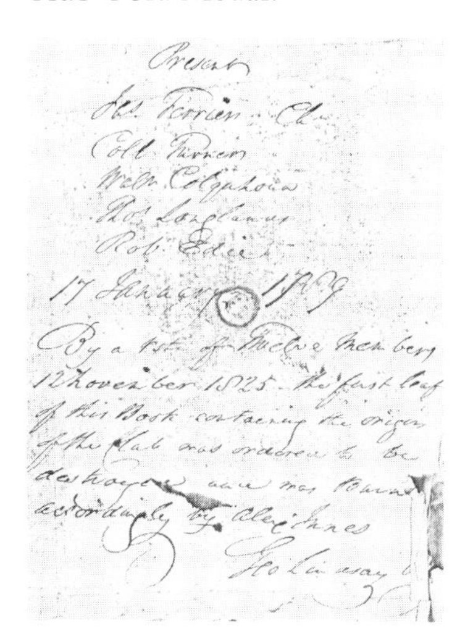

Present
Jas. Torrie Ch
Coll Torrie
Walt Colquhoun
Robt Longlands
Robt Edie
17 January 1789
By a vote of twelve members 12 November 1825 the first leaf of this Book containing the origin of the Club was ordered to be destroyed and was torn accordingly by Alex Innes
Geo Lindsay

The first existing page of the Knuckle Club Minute Book (page 5), the first four pages having been removed

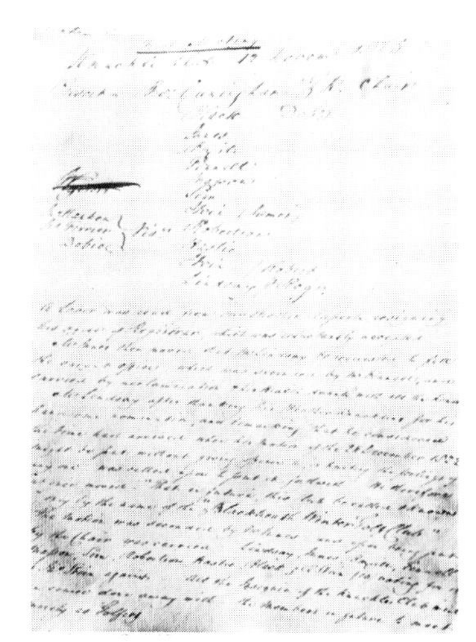

Knuckle Club Minute Book – 12 November 1825 with the final phrase 'The members in future to meet as golfers'

The Knuckle Club Medal 1789

The reason given by Hughes, the author of the *Chronicles*, for the missing minutes prior to 1800 was 'an ever to be lamented fire at the end of the last century'. In the first place, if there was a fire, how did the items listed above all survive and, secondly, there is no reference in any of the minutes to any such fire affecting damage to their property or their meeting place–the Green Man, which inevitably would have been mentioned. The truth must be that the minutes were destroyed, in a similar manner to the other contemporary Scottish Societies, in order to preserve their secrets, and as done later by the Knuckle Club itself.

The destruction of the minutes suggests an earlier masonic background of the membership and our attention must first centre on an unusually interesting figure, the first recorded Captain of the Club in 1766, and again in 1767–one Alexander Duncan of Craigton, Scotland.* He had already been Captain of the Royal and Ancient in 1756 and 1761 (and was once more in 1791), see below. His presence is recorded at Leith in 1767 at the laying of the foundation stone of the new Clubhouse by the Grandmaster Mason of Scotland and he is mentioned in the minutes of the Edinburgh Company as being Captain of Blackheath and a master mason. He was also to become Captain of the Edinburgh Company in 1771–a unique record. So here we have a man, known to be a mason, who was fully familiar with

* Alexander Duncan was the son of James Duncan, Professor of Philosophy at St Andrews. He was admitted advocate on 5 August 1755, married Margaret Dalrymple, daughter of Colonel Campbell Dalrymple on 5 January 1781 and died on 23 January 1799. (*Faculty of Advocates in Scotland 1532–1943*, p.61, Scottish Record Society)

the organisation and customs of two leading Scottish Societies at that time.

Looking, as we are, for an explanation of Blackheath being 'instituted in 1608', it was hoped that masonic rather than golfing history might provide some clues and fresh research may yet reveal something. 'Speculative Masonry' did not get under way until the beginning of the eighteenth century and it is asking a lot to trace a link with 1608 through the troubled years of the seventeenth century. Golf, however, did arrive at Blackheath in 1603 or thereabouts and somehow it did survive and appeared again in the mid-eighteenth century. We know that golf was being played at Tothill Fields, Westminster, London, obviously by Scots, in 1658 (see p. 4) and the many Scottish expatriates in London together with the occupants of the great houses adjacent to Blackheath could well have kept it going and eventually provided a nucleus for renewed activity in the eighteenth century. For instance, one member of James I's Court who came south with him in 1603, was Patrick Maule* a Gentleman of the Bedchamber. Around 1620 he was appointed Keeper of Eltham Park, adjacent to Blackheath. In July 1842 when the first proposal was made to change the course from 5 holes to 7, it was proposed by the Hon. Robert Fox Maule (Captain in 1844 and 1845). So here is a descendant of one of the original families who came south, being associated with the early moves to improve the course (see Chapter 1).

There can be no question that Blackheath was the first recorded golfing ground outside Scotland, and there can be little doubt that we owe the establishment of organised golf at Blackheath to the freemasons. It was entirely in keeping with their movement at that time to hallow it with ancient inspiration; and it is not surprising that they should seek to commemorate the start of golf at Blackheath (although no explanation can be offered for choosing 1608 and not 1603) with an Anniversary Day going back to the beginning. It was to be the important event in the Club's year when guests were always entertained. The earliest notice about this event dates from 9 August 1785 in the *Public Advertiser*:

> 'Goff Club
> Assembly House, Blackheath
>
> The Anniversary of the Society is appointed to be held at this House, on Saturday next, the 13th instant, when the SILVER CLUB will be played for. Such Members as mean to accompany the Captain to the Heath, are requested to be punctual to the hour of twelve o'clock.
>
> Dinner on Table exactly at Four.'

* Patrick Maule created Earl of Panmure in 1646 had been a boyhood companion to James VI. He was a Gentleman of the Bedchamber to both James I and Charles I.

From then on it can be traced through the account books up to 1800 and thereafter (apart from war years) down to the present day, the Anniversary of 1608 is remembered by that inspired phrase 'instituted 1608'.* There are some who will say that the link the founding fathers 'instituted' was more romantic than factual; but a nearly 200 year-old tradition has now endowed Blackheath with the year 1608 and long may it continue to do so. (See Chapter 11.)

Associated with the Annual Day was the Silver Club dated 1766, which is not considered to have any particular significance associated with its date other than introducing competitive golf as a means of choosing a Captain and thus recording his name on a silver ball. The Silver Club is not only the oldest relic but is first referred to in a notice in the press on 9 August 1785 (already referred to). We do not know the exact condition under which Mr Foot gave the club and no Rules of Golf for regulating play are mentioned. Until 1802 it would appear that, on the Annual or Anniversary Day, the members played in a stroke competition to decide who was to be Captain or Chairman of the Club for the following year. From 1782–1808 the members elected a Captain and the 1805 minutes record that Mr Youille was 'inducted with the usual ceremonies and took the customary oaths accordingly'. From 1808 to 1822 they played again for the Silver Club but then gave it up and annually elected the new Chairman and provided a Summer Medal to be played for instead. Thereafter the Silver Club continued to have silver balls attached to it by the Captain who held it for his year of office. Unfortunately not only are three balls missing with the names of the Captains on them in 1775, 1778 and 1779, but in the first hundred years there are only 69 balls attached. The Silver Club required £8.10.0, spending on it in 1790 and almost immediately afterwards they sold five 'old silver balls' for 2 gns.

The Silver Club itself was a copy of a play club or driver (unlike the Edinburgh and R. & A. clubs which were models of putters) and was made of low-grade silver and therefore not hallmarked. The balls were not solid silver but ordinary feathery balls coated with silver and some of the early ones carried the coats of arms of the respective Captains. In 1831 Captain Boxall altered the method of affixing the balls to the club, so that more balls could be attached. In due course two further silver clubs were acquired in order to maintain the role of Captains down to the present day.

There was, besides the Captain, another officer, the Field Marshal (whom today we would call the President) whose office goes back to earliest days. How and why the title came to be used remains a mystery, because it has, until now, been assumed that his function was to 'marshal the field' when stroke play was first introduced (i.e. playing for the Silver Club). This would appear

* 12 March 1831. To ensure the insertion of Blackheath Golf Club in the *Edinburgh Almanack*–with the date of 1608. 12 copies are to be ordered annually at 1s. 6d. each. The Almanack had been in the habit of publishing a list of the leading golfing societies and the foundation dates they claimed.

to pre-empt the job of the Captain whose custom it was to lead out the players to the first tee (see p. 29). The rank of Field Marshal in the British Army dates from January 1736 when George Earl of Orkney and John Duke of Argyll were both promoted to that rank.

The first-known holder of the title of Field Marshal was a Mr John Walker of Point House, Blackheath, who in 1802 was invested with a special golf medal to be worn at all golf dinners and special occasions and thereafter recorded the names of all who have held the office. We do not know when Mr Walker was appointed but the medal was presented for long and meretorious service to the Club and he was not necessarily the first. His uniform was distinguished because he always wore two epaulettes, one on each shoulder, whereas the Captain wore just one (on the right shoulder)–and past-Captains none. The origin of this strange custom is unknown. Appearing un-epauletted merited the usual fine and is recorded both against a Field Marshal and a Captain (5 April 1806). The death of a Field Marshal was mourned by each member wearing crepe on the field and at the dining table for the remainder of the season. The new Field Marshal was always installed with due ceremony.

The position is further confused by the title of Captain General, confirmed on Henry Callender in June 1807 (see p. 113). Captain General was not a rank but a title bestowed upon George Monck Duke of Albemarle in 1660. The last to hold the appointment seems to have been the Duke of York in 1799, who had already been promoted to the rank of Field Marshal in 1795.

Henry Callender paid a fine of £21 on behalf of a Mr Campbell for not accepting the Captain Generalship in August 1794.

The Knuckle Club
(1789–1825)

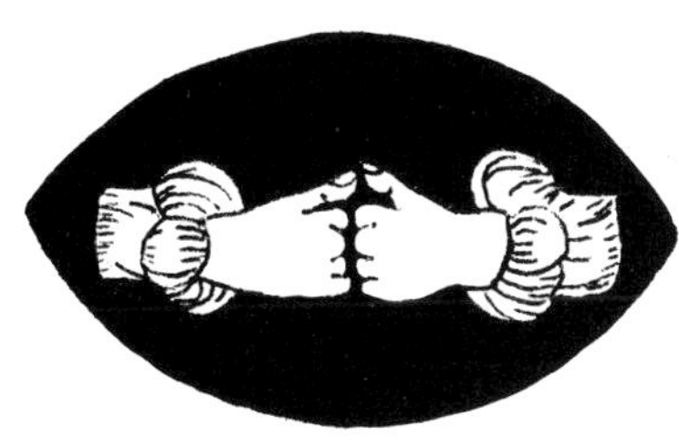

Human knuckles – sketch taken from the centre design of the Knuckle Club Medal

If any confirmation were needed of the mystic origins of the Blackheath Club it is provided by the minutes of the Knuckle Club which was founded on 17 January 1789, as a separate Winter Club, but acknowledged the Blackheath Club–now referred to as the Summer Club–as the parent Club. The minutes are remarkably complete, only the first four pages covering six of the first 22 Regulations being cut out and destroyed, together with the insignia when the Club was wound up in 1825. This was a masonic lodge, whose minutes are of considerable importance in throwing light on the origins of organised golf; but why was it formed? The reason must lie in the increasing admission of non-mason members to the parent Club. We suspect the existence of the problem in the Scottish Clubs, but here at Blackheath a way was found of satisfying the needs of those who wanted to continue to practise the craft in the Club and were prepared to accept the dropping of the qualification in the parent Club. It is interesting that they had their own Anniversary Day–not an exact date as they moved from one in January to March–and furthermore there were a number of the prominent members who held office in both Clubs. It was extraordinary that, even after the winding up of the Knuckle Club in 1825, the Winter Club should be formed to take its place and continue a separate existence for another 18 years. The 'Green Man Knuckle', as it was also known, does not appear in London masonic records, but the Club was small and had this peculiar addiction to winter golf.

Hughes stated in his *Chronicles* that he could understand that some golfers might want to play golf throughout the winter months, because the Blackheath Club started the season at the beginning of April and ended it on the first Saturday in November. He expressed himself as being completely baffled as to the reasons for which it was formed and comments on the fact that one had to go through several pages of minutes before there is any mention of golf.

The minutes are contained in two ordinary notebooks, the pages being numbered. The title page has, what we know from a subsequent insertion to be, the letters 'C.-T.' which have been cut out. The date is 17 January 1789 and this is followed by the toasts:

The King
Knuckle
The Butcher's wife by the Dept. [The Deputy Chairman]

The first four pages of the minutes were, as we shall describe, cut out and destroyed when the Club was wound up in 1825. These pages contained six of the first 22 Regulations which outlined the initiation ceremony, and the first surviving page reads as follows:

'. . . Register is to read or tell the story, instruct him in the sign, the order to be delivered him, and Then he is to be introduced to all the Members present.

7th
That we do continue to meet in the Knuckle Green Man Blackheath every Saturday until April next at the Meeting of the Golf Club, when the Members of the Knuckle will fix a proper day for their Meeting.

8th
That in honor of the Blackheath Golf Club (of which most of us are Members) we do make it a Rule that any Member thereof wishing to become a Knuckle be balloted for first Meeting at Club hours.

9th
That any person who wishes to become a Member of the

Knuckle, and is not a Member of the Blackheath Golf Club, must dine with us one Saturday previous to being proposed.

10th
That no person shall be present while the Members are Balloting for him.

11th
That each Member may invite two friends on any club day, and to have it in his option to pay or not for them.

12th
That the Landlord do provide a dish of Soup and Knuckles (particularly Beef Ones) for six Members at 1/6 per Head every Saturday at 4 o'clock, that money to be paid by the Register.

13th
That this Society do always adjourn at 6 o'clock at which time the Bill is to be called for.

14th
That 5 Members do constitute a Club and elect Members, etc.

15th
That no Member shall signify any kind of displeasure if the Gentleman he proposes shall be Blackball'd, and that he shall take no notice whatever thereof.

16th
That the duties of Chair and Deputy shall continue for one meeting only, and that previous to adjournment, the Deputy shall name his Successor who must accept, or give a satisfactory reason for his refusal.

17th
That no Member shall speak on matters relating to the Club longer than 5 minutes, during which time he is to hold the Knuckle in his right hand.

18th
That any Member attempting to speak (without the Knuckle in his right hand) on the business of the Club (except the Chair) shall be fined as the Chairman shall think fit.

19th
That we begin to Ballot for Members and do any other Business the Club may require immediately after drinking the third Bumper after dinner.

20th
That all visitors do withdraw during the new Members' initiation.

21st
That immediately upon the adjournment of the Club, each Member do deliver his ornaments into the hands of the Register, who is carefully to lock them up till following meeting.

22nd
That no Member shall be call'd to serve as Chair, Deputy or Register, if he has served before in the Season, unless every Member present is in the same predicament with himself.'

Further Regulations were added during the year as follows:

'23rd
That the number of this shall be limited to Thirty Members.

24th
That in future no Gentleman who shall be Balloted for, can be considered a Member, unless he appears at the Club the second meeting after, or assign a Reason satisfactory to the Society.

25th
That when a Member is proposed and seconded the Proposer or Seconder shall be present on the day of Balloting, or the Saturday following, and should neither of the Parties attend, the Gentleman proposed shall for that time be withdrawn, and before being Balloted for again, be regularly proposed and seconded, subject to the present of the partys before mentioned.

26th
That no stranger who is not a member of the Golf Club, shall from this day be proposed a Member of the Knuckle for the season.

27th
That Mr. Edie not having appeared as Chairman elected for this day, Mr. Turner to take the Chair–Mr. Alder Deputy. The meeting appointed Mr. Alder to succeed as Chair next meeting and to name his Deputy at next meeting when the Company shall assemble. This resolution to be a precedent.

28th
That any Member belonging to this Club residing in or near London, and not attending or assigning a sufficient reason for his absence on or before the 17th January next, being the anniversary of its institution, shall not thereafter be considered a Member, and shall be for ever excluded from becoming a Member or Visitor of the Club.

29th
That the Anniversary of the 17th January being the day of the Institution of this Club be held on every succeeding 17th January, if a Saturday, or if the 17th is on any other day in the week, the Anniversary be held on the Saturday following.

30th
That no Visitor shall appear in the Club above two Club days in the Season. Excepting Gentlemen from abroad, or whose general Residence is distant from London.

Resolved that the Register be directed to send to each Member of the Club, a copy of the first resolution of this day.

Limited number of Club full. Honorary Members elected, to come up for election in rotation.

31st
Resolved that during the Season of the Knuckle Club, Dinner be ordered to be on the Table punctually at ½ past 3 o'clock.

18th Dec. 1790
Every member may be allowed to invite his friends to the Anniversary and that this be a Standing Rule.'

(Note: 8th Jan. 1791 The Anniversary was advertised in the *Times* and the *Gazetteer*)

We have the list of 55 members of the Blackheath Club in 1787 and of these 19 became Knuckle Club members. Of these 19, six (James Ferrier, Coll Turner, Thomas Longlands, Robert Edie, Charles Graham and Henry Callender) were not initiated and

Green Man Hotel and Tavern, taken from an unknown print c. 1860

were presumably already qualified to join because the other 13 members of the Blackheath Club were all elected and subsequently noted in the minutes as having been initiated. A gentleman called Mr Walter Colquhoun appears as the only original founder member not belonging to the Blackheath Club and he was not initiated, so was presumably already qualified. The breakaway to form a secret sporting and dining club clearly attracted some support from the parent Club including that of the illustrious Henry Callender (see his portrait on p.18) who was Secretary of the Blackheath Club in 1788/9 and Captain in 1790 and 1807. In a minute dated 23 January 1790 both he and Mr Dunlop were thrown out for non-attendance of the Knuckle Anniversary meeting and 'forever excluded from becoming members or visitors of the Club'. During the life of the Knuckle Club there are not more than three or four other cases for dismissal for non-attendance,* but it is on the strength of the minute against an officer of the so-called parent Club which indicates that the relationship was not as cordial as it might have been. As we have said we can only assume that the Knuckle Club came into being to satisfy a desire amongst some of its members to continue what Hughes termed the mystic elements and qualifications, which were gradually being dropped by the parent Club.

The Club met every Saturday at the Green Man, Blackheath, and referred to itself as the 'Green Man Knuckle'. On 31 January 1789 the cash book records the purchase of 'one new hammer [there are still two surviving with "Knuckle" inscribed on them], 10 bones, ribbons, etc. for 14s 6d.' Knuckle bones were thereafter the insignia of the Club and members were forbidden to leave the

* but on 27 June 1798 it was resolved that anyone so excluded should be reinstated on receipt of a written apology.

room wearing them. At the same time it was laid down that they dined upon the dish of soup and knuckles every Saturday at 4 o'clock. Some years later (1808) they got tired of this and resolved to have it on the last Saturday in the Season only. We cannot but wonder at the significance of knuckle bones–that they should use them as 'insignia' and also dine upon a dish of Knuckles. Note also the human Knuckle design of the Gold Medal. (The beef knuckle bone is huge and at least 12–18 inches long. It could hardly be worn. Veal or lamb bones seem a more probable size, see Regulation 18–the Knuckle had to be held in the right hand in order to speak.)

In 1815 Colonel Nordenfelt, a Hanoverian officer and Governor of Wolfenbüttel Castle (see page 50), was elected and an honorary bone was awarded. Two years later 'Mr. Lindsay took away a bone to be repaired and beautified for the purpose of being transmitted to our brother Colonel Nordenfelt'. As late as 28 December 1822 Brother Croft offered to present a new set of Ribbons for the Insignia of the Club and the Registrar was requested to send all the bones sealed up to Brother Croft's house. A week later they were back and Mrs Croft and her ladies who helped were rewarded by their health being drunk–'a bumper'.

A new member first of all dined with the Club and was later initiated and both attendances are recorded, as also are comments such as '29 December 1804–after a severe examination . . . passed the ordeal bravely' '1810 24 November Dr. George Young was initiated and passed the sign in style' and a little later '20 February 1813 Capt. Henry Sturrock RN (1774–1844) proposed as a brother Golfer was elected, initiated and passed in style, almost answering the sign and question'. (This may have some significance as indicating that not all the members were golfers.) Another member was elected, initiated and passed in the most extraordinary style–a committee to examine and report (7 January 1815). By 1820 a motion to dispense with the ceremony of initiation was defeated by four votes to one but by 1822 it was left to the discretion of the Registrar.

The bets were all entered in the minutes and the proceeds all went to the Club. The fines–usually a gallon of claret–value a guinea–reduced the wine bill and were also recorded. Anyone who married or fathered a child also paid up–the entry in the minute book varying in terminology. 'Bro. John McKenzie . . . . The Lady and Younkers health drunk in a brimmer' (14 November 1801). James Walker 'The Lady and young Infidel's health were drunk in a Bumper' (21 January 1804) and again Bro. James Walker this time has a son 'The Lady in the straw and the Young Knuckler's health drunk in a Bumper' (15 November 1806). 22 November 1820 'Grand Knuckle' Leslie Finlayson (Grand because he had won the Medal) paid up 3 gallons on his marriage; and on 23 January 1823 'Mr. Finlayson presented the

Club with a gallon on the birth of a daughter and the Health of the Lady in the Straw was drunk in a Bumper. The Sovereign was spent in this days Bill'. In February 1824 he paid another gallon for the birth of a son, and then most unfortunately lost one of his feet, being thrown off the stage (coach) through the carelessness and obstinacy of a Greenwich stage-coach driver. The Club refused to accept his subscription for the ensuing season.,

As to golf, they made use of the parent Club's holecutter and professional for his services paying whenever they used him for laying out the holes, and from the cashbook during those winter months it does not appear that he was all that often called upon. They did not specifically adopt any rules or regulations for the conduct of their games. They then decided to have a Gold Medal: a glance at the illustration on p. 28 shows two fists or knuckles as the centre piece, and this must have some relevance to the activities of the Club. The design was finally decided upon on 24 March 1792 and they played for it a week later. It cost £5 5s and must have been made in a week. The winner had his name engraved on it for 2s and was then entitled to be called the Grand Knuckle. This Medal is the oldest in golfing history and has engraved on it the names of no less than 175 winners dating from 1792. The inscription is 'quaesitum vitrice manu' which perhaps may be freely translated as 'Reward of skilled victory'. In 1771 the R. & A. were the first actually to play for a Gold Medal which was apparently won outright and their next Gold Medal did not appear until 1805 and was then for annual competition.

Strangely the first winning score over the course of 5 holes played three times (i.e. 15 holes) was not recorded and this happened on six other occasions. The lowest score was 110–the average between 125 and 130, with one high score of 148 in 1819. The number of entrants was rarely given (in 1817 there were four) but there cannot have been more than a handful although they also had scrutineers and in March 1804 after 'careful and impartial examination' declared Mr Peter Lawrie winner with 132 and Mr Christie with 145. Another card was presented but 'it appearing that the Gentleman had only went two rounds' they could not take any notice thereof. The golfing activities were frequently affected by bad weather but various matches on which bets were laid are recorded in the minutes and mostly involved some form of handicap. They were similar in form to those of the Summer Club, examples of which are given later on.

In November 1790 a Uniform Sub-committee met at the London Tavern to decide upon the kind of uniform to be worn but thereafter there is no information as to what they had agreed on. Unlike other Golfing Societies of the time no requirements were laid down by the Club that uniform must be worn on certain occasions.

The early enthusiasm for weekly meetings declined after a few years and by February 1793 there were fewer than five members present. If it was fine they played golf and had dinner but no ceremonies and there was no Club meeting as such. By 1795 the weekly meetings had dwindled and there were only six members present at the Anniversary, although in 1800 there were still 30 members of whom 11 had not paid their subscriptions. In comparison, the Summer Club membership had fallen to thirty-seven. Thereafter weekly meetings continued to be poorly attended and by 1820 the membership was down to eleven and the subscription was reduced from £2 2s to £1 10s. Blackheath had by then only twenty-two members. On 12 November 1825 Mr Lindsay, having been elected Registrar of the Knuckle Club, moved that his original resolution of 28 December 1822 which was that the Club be called the Winter Club and in fact wound up, be put again 'without giving offence to or hurting the feelings of anyone'.

The resolution ended with the following significant sentence 'The Members in future to meet merely as golfers'. This was carried by ten votes to one. It was then that the first four pages of the minutes were cut out, the insignia were destroyed and the Knuckle Club came to an end.

The Winter Club then took over, starting with sixteen subscribers in 1826 (the Summer Club now had twenty-three members). The Gold Medal continued to be played for but was now called the Spring Medal and between 1826 and 1842 only five different winners' names appear on it–Mr G. C. Anderson winning eight times in succession between 1835 and 1842. In 1843, for reasons which are given later, the Club for the first time tried out the new Hazard 7-hole course, just before it was wound up. The Winter Club slowly declined in popularity, finally ending with only eight members, but it is interesting that in 1832 there was a proposal that they should acquire their own Clubhouse.

The Blackheath Golf Club–The 'Summer Club'
(1787–1843)

The account books and the bets book survive from 1787 and tell us something about the activities of the Summer Club before the minutes began in 1800. They start with a list of the members–fifty-five in number paying £2. 2s. each. The Captain was Coll Turner, the Secretary Henry Callender and the Treasurer Charles Kensington–a very Sassenach name for the treasurer of a Scottish Club to have. The name of William Innes appears next, the subject of probably one of the best-known portraits in the history of golf.

Painted by Lemuel Francis Abbott RA (1760–1803) in 1790, the original has been lost. The earliest engraving was by Valentine Green and was dedicated to the Society of Golfers at Blackheath in 1793. William Innes is shown on the Heath, with Morden

College and Shooters Hill in the background together with one of the windmills. He is dressed in the uniform as Captain, with one epaulette, and his caddie is dressed in the uniform of a Pensioner of the Royal Naval Hospital, Greenwich–the pensioners were known in the Club as the 'College men'.*

Not quite so well known is the portrait which hangs in the Clubhouse, also by L. F. Abbott, RA, of the Secretary (1787), Captain in 1790, 1801 and 1807, that of Henry Callender. When he took the Chair as Captain on 11 June 1807, Mr Walker assisted by Mr Lawrie took the opportunity of expressing the regard and affection of the Club to the Chairman by placing upon his shoulder an additional epaulette, and his health under the appellation of 'Captain General' was drunk with great applause. He died the following year. It will be noticed that in his portrait he has epaulettes on both shoulders. There is no explanation for the title of Captain General and it was not used again until Mr Guy T. Eagleton was appointed in 1973 [Captain in 1937 and senior past-Captain but at his wish never Field Marshal] (see p. 113). The club leaning against the table to his left is referred to on page 132 and is probably that in the Club collection.

Of the membership list of fifty-five in 1787 at least thirty were merchants or brokers in the City or West End of London. Some twenty of the members can be traced as having residences at Blackheath. These were all on the west side of the Heath, where the Green Man Tavern, the Club's meeting place, was also situated.

Some of the members in the 1787 list

Coll Turner A committee member of the Club and a merchant with a West Indies connection: he traded from Brabant Court in the City of London.

Arthur and Robert Edie were merchants trading as Edie & Laird at No. 5 Token House Yard, Lothbury in the City of London. They presented a pair of gavels to the Club (see illustration on p. 27).

Captain Edward Addison a merchant and insurance broker of No. 34 Bread Street in the City of London.

Gordon Urquart a wine merchant of Villiers Street, Charing Cross in the West End of London.

Robert Oliphant of 2 London Street in the City was a broker.

Patrick McLeod Lived in the Grove, Blackheath and traded as a merchant in Bread Street in the City of London.

Thomas Mure Broker of Mure & Atkinson, 32 Fenchurch Street in the City of London.

* William Innes (1719–1795) (Captain of the Club 1778) of Lime Street, London & Blackheath, MP for Ilchester 1774–1775. Son of Alexander Innes of Cathlowm, West Lothian, Banker and Merchant of Edinburgh. In 1749 Innes was established as a London merchant trading with the West Indies where he had extensive family connections. He had a house at Blackheath and is buried at St Andrews Undershaft in the corner of Leadenhall Street and St Mary Axe in the the City and in the church there is a large memorial plaque to him. He died without issue.

Memorial plaque to William Innes at St Andrews Undershaft, St Mary Axe, London

Alexander Shairp of Shairp Maud & Co. Russia merchants, in the City of London.

Alderman George M. Macauley a City of London Alderman who lived at a house called Dartmouth Hill House, Blackheath. This property was substantial with a six-horse stable, hot houses and an ice house.

Alexander Dalrymple A man of this name was Master to the Charts of the East India Company in the 1780s. Many members of the East India Company and their fleet captains lived at Blackheath at this period.

William Dunbar probably of Dunbar & McCormick, merchants and stockbrokers, 15 Token House Yard, Lothbury in the City of London.

James Duff a merchant of 9 Salisbury Street, Strand, West End of London.

James Lindsay merchant of Nicholas Lane, Lombard Street, City of London.

In the 1800s even more of the Club membership was made up of local men as new building developments were completed, such as Montpelier Row and The Paragon at Blackheath.

Sir Robert Stewart who died in 1804 was the first resident of Paragon House in 1797 and joined the Golf Club that year. He had a West Indies connection and his wife Elizabeth was described as a 'West Indian Woman!'

J. B. Duncan lived in Montpelier Row and the tenancy of his house was taken over by Edward Eagleton (1786–1860) an antecedent of the present Captain General Guy Eagleton.

Alexander Campell lived at No. 8 Montpelier Row Blackheath. From this house Sir John Douglas spied on Caroline of Brunswick and took tales back to the Prince of Wales' staff about her irregular behaviour. He appears as a guest at the Golf Club.

The minutes (1800–1843)

They record the Chairman of the day, usually the Captain, names of all the other members present and any visitors, together with the activities of the Club on the green and in the clubroom, and they are supplemented by account books. With play being held on 35 Saturdays in the year, they are extensive but not copious and they give the bare facts of eating and drinking the toasts and the result of the golf, if there is a Medal Day, but no more.

Unhappily there is little description of the game of golf as they were playing it: this Club required organisation, remembering that there was no office equipment or telephone in those days, but there was a degree of discipline about their affairs–disguised if you like by fines of a gallon of claret, which kept them going.

Along with the toasts was the customary singing, and if a guest performed well it was acknowledged in the minutes. In the fly leaves of the Club copy of Thomas Mathison's *The Goff* (2nd edition 1793) five golfing songs are recorded, which were sung at Club dinners. William Jerdan 1782–1869 from Kelso in Scotland was a distinguished writer, a member of the Club to whom he dedicated a song (July 1817) which begins–Verse 1:

> 'Let us chaunt a famed pastime, debased by no scoff,
> Of life that grand emblem, our favourite Golf;
> Though when all our hazards and best strokes are past
> Death comes–the sure Putter–and holes us at last;
> With his Fol de rol etc'

A Mr C. R. Broughton a member of the Club wrote another song in 1826 about a new Club on Brighton Downs.
Verse 1:

> 'From London some Sons of auld Reekie set off
> To establish at Brighton a wee Club of Golf
> The Downs near this place are just the right sort
> For enjoying *con gusto* that elegant sport.'

and the song ends

> 'Huzza here's good luck to the new Brighton Club
> I hope their success will not meet with a rub.'

and is perhaps evidence of early missionary zeal by some of its members. There was another song, 'The Golfers' Garland', which was composed for the Blackheath Golf Club and must have been written prior to 1793 as it is printed in the Appendix to Thomas Mathison's *Goff* mentioned above. The importance of the songs can also be gauged by the fact that Mr Thomas Marsh who was a member in the 1880s was regarded as the Club's poet laureate and his collection of poems about golf were published at the expense of the Club.

To anyone reading the minutes for the first time, they would not place golf as the first objective. It was the dinner, the company, the songs, the conviviality and the entertainment of guests. Golf triumphed in the end when the regular dining had been relaxed and the release from this commitment for every Saturday did at any rate return the player sometimes to his home and family in time for a late dinner.

'The Green Man', Blackheath. Rebuilt in 1869 and finally demolished in 1974 (see p.5)

The first description of golf on the Heath comes from a newspaper cutting in Greenwich Public Library dated 1787:

> 'On Saturday a fine game of Goff was played upon Blackheath, by upwards of thirty gentlemen of the London Scots Society, dressed in uniforms, in scarlet jackets, and white waistcoats. The fineness of the day, and the picturesque appearance of the players, with their attendants in blue, continually moving in small parties all over the heath, rendered it a sight highly pleasing. The excellency of this ancient North British game, is that the players are in continual exercise; whilst, at the same time, their minds are always intent upon the distances which they must accomplish with their balls. Not the least pleasant part of it, is, that the game is so plain, that it is impossible any disputes can arise, with respect to the decision,–The party played till three o'clock, and then retired to dinner, at the Coffee-house upon the heath.'

There is no explanation for the term–'London Scots Society'.

A day's golf at Blackheath at the turn of the eighteenth century and thereafter, would start with the necessity, if you lived in the City of London, of getting down there by 12 o'clock ready to play. Some had villas at Blackheath or nearby, such as William Innes; some may have used their own carriage and others would have used the public coach service to the Green Man Hotel and Tavern, which was on the west end of the Heath and, as the population grew, developed into an important coaching centre. Not only did coaches for East Kent stop there, but by the 1830s there were no less than three regular coach services terminating there; two from Gracechurch Street in the City and one from Charing Cross. (The type of coach used by the Charing Cross

Blackheath coach, a T. H. Shepherd print showing a Blackheath coach outside Northumberland House, Charing Cross, 1830

Company.) Thus throughout the day there were, by then, coaches leaving for London every quarter of an hour. Our golfers were well served.

Advertisements in newspapers were the accepted method of communication with members and a notice of 9 August 1788 announced: 'Such members as mean to accompany the Captain to the Heath are requested to be punctual to the hour of twelve o'clock. Dinner on table exactly at four.' (This seems to imply that not all the members necessarily went out to play the full 3 rounds.) The meal was punctually ended at 6 p.m. to enable them to catch a coach back and this is sometimes noted in the minutes.

No hint is given as to whether the members kept their uniform at the Green Man and changed into it on arrival and again on leaving, but we assume that they did. Their clubs would have all been kept down at Blackheath, so members would be travelling light and, on arrival, they probably ate something and were then ready for play at twelve o'clock, having walked from the Green Man to the Club tent, erected adjacent to the first tee (see pp. 58–9) or assembly area.

In the mean time the course had been prepared. It was 5 holes, laid out over that part of the Heath which was not affected by gravel pits, some of which were then being worked, and it remained in this form until 1843, when the new Hazard Course of 7 holes was introduced. Unfortunately no record of the layout of the course survives. The terrain was covered with scrub, bracken and whins or gorse, and some of the grass was kept down by grazing animals and never grew to such length in the summer as to interfere with play as later happened on inland courses. It was however by no means ideal golfing ground.

From the earliest time Blackheath employed a clubmaker, the first-recorded being one Donaldson who was paid an annual retainer of £10 plus an additional fee when he also cut the holes. With over fifty members each playing with a set maybe of eight clubs and owning more, he was probably looking after well over 500 clubs. He would be kept busy just maintaining those clubs, but we do not know to what extent he or any of the later professionals down until 1844 actually made clubs, and there are no surviving examples attributed to a known clubmaker.* Mortality amongst wooden clubs was heavy–seaside links were far kinder than the stony Heath. Donaldson, who died in 1815, was followed by Ballantyne, Cockburn in 1821, Poke and then Archibald Sharpe in 1823. There is a watercolour sketch of 'Corporal' Sharpe on the Heath dated 1833 where he appears with a white top hat. He died in 1834. This recently-discovered sketch is fittingly matched by Old Alick's portrait.

Various holecutters were employed until eventually a regular man was used–the most famous being Old Alick (1756–1840).

He went to sea at the age of 13 from Leith, and on the back of the portrait in his own handwriting he put the names of the ships in which he had served during the late war and their captains.

The professional was responsible then for seeing that five 'Guardians of the Green' went out to the 5 holes, each carrying a flagstick to put in the hole which they guarded whilst play was in progress. We have always been curious to know when the first flagsticks were used for marking the hole and now we find from the early records that at Blackheath they were in use and there are bills for repairing 'the staves and the flags'. They were not left out unattended and the Club was lucky to have these uniformed attendants, paid 1s each for their afternoon's work. They were the Greenwich Pensioners (always referred to as the Greenwich men or College men) in the uniform depicted in the illustration on page 17 and others of their number were caddies. Re-echoing the earlier journalist's comment in 1785–with players and caddies in uniform it must have been an impressive sight as they all gathered at the tent and then set off round the course. In later years, you can see in the background to Old Alick's portrait how the fashion in hats has changed. Not only is he wearing a white top hat (slightly battered) but so are the players. The Heath was a windswept place. We know by the windmills that used to stand there, and whatever the current fashion–William Innes-style or Old Alick and Corporal Sharpe (see p. 24)-style, it must have been hard to keep your hat on and strike the ball.

* McEwan, the Bruntsfield, Edinburgh, clubmaker was said to have had an agent at Blackheath in the early 1800s.

The matches that were to be played were sometimes arranged as the result of bets made at previous dinners and recorded, and were on similar lines to those of the Knuckle Club, some having nothing to do with the game. Here are examples of general bets:

1 **9 July 1791**
Mr Loughnan bets Mr A. S. Gordon one gallon claret that it is not lawful to purchase Stock of the Holder while that Stock is shut for paying the dividend. Mr Barnes and Mr Platt both eminent Stockbrokers gave their opinion–that buying Stock when it could not be delivered was a TIME BARGAIN, consequently not lawful.

2 **1 June 1793**
Mr Morgan bets Mr Glasgow two gallons of claret to one that Tobago was not in possession of the British on 26 April 1793. (Note: Tobago was captured by Gen. Cuyler on 15 April and the news arrived in London on the day the bet was lost.)

3 **13 July 1805**
Mr Jas. Walker bets Mr Broughton a gallon that Lord Nelson comes up with the French fleet before they reach port either in America or Europe.

4 **12 July 1808**
Mr Ruperti bets Mr Callender a gallon that Jerôme Bonaparte is brought a prisoner into England before he returns to France.

5 **5 January 1811**
Capt. Simpson with Walker. 2 guineas. CRIB shall beat MOLINEUX when they next fight (prize).

6 **7 December 1822**
Mr Black Sen. lays a gallon against Mr James Stein that he will break a broomstick suspended between two bumpers of wine, without spilling the wine or breaking the glasses. Lost by Mr James Stein.

The idea of a medal round had been instituted by the Knuckle Club in 1792, but as the Summer Club had only the Silver Club to play for (and that spasmodically) until the Summer Medal in 1823 (see page 47), the occasions for stroke play competition were rare and the idea of a handicap by means of the number of strokes or holes given or received to an opponent was still some way off. Stroke play usually involved three scrutineers and a card, but only much later (Medal Day 7 June 1834) when there were two scrutineers and fifteen entries do we learn that:

> 'After Dinner the Scrutineers retired to examine the cards of the Candidates, and make up the Report of the days play. Upon the Report being presented to the Secretary, being a revision upon their scrutiny upon the Green, the result of the play was as follows . . . Mr. Dunbar and Mr. Hastie each 109.'

Anyway Hastie and Dunbar were made to play off the tie with a 'half round' and again tied and were sent out to play another 'half round' before Mr Hastie won by a stroke. These were good scores by two consistent players and they were set out in the minutes:

Hastie	8	5	8	7	7	=	35
	9	10	7	7	6	=	39
	8	7	7	7	6	=	35
							109
Dunbar	8	7	6	8	7	=	36
	7	8	6	8	8	=	37
	8	10	6	6	6	=	36
							109

They were sent out to play a half round

Hastie	5	7	5	=	17
Dunbar	5	7	5	=	17

and then another

Hastie	5	8	6	=	19
Dunbar	6	8	6	=	20

so Hastie won.

There are references from time to time to the 'short holes' which are believed to have been adjacent to the first tee or assembly point and the equivalent of today's Clubhouse putting green. The half round with two of the holes played in five strokes and reference to a 'short hole in' may well have been contrived in conjunction with the so-called 'short holes'. There is mention at various times to the 'Assembly Rooms hole' probably the last one in, and another 'Shooters Hill', and there were two points on the course called 'Thorntree' and 'Braehead' named after holes on the Leith course at Edinburgh which also had 5 holes and 'short holes'.

The winning scores for the Medal round over the years were no doubt influenced by weather conditions–the feathery ball performed badly when it got wet and wheezed through the air. The scores for the Spring Medal (1825–1842) varied 103–124. The Summer Medal scores 1825–1843 were 102–113, and that medal played for in June produced consistently lower scores over the years in what must have been better weather conditions. The highest winning score for any medal was 148 in 1819 for the Knuckle Medal. The following are examples of some of the bets on golf:

1 **22 January 1791**
Mr Turner bets Mr Walker one gallon of claret that he beats him three holes in 4 rounds, Mr Walker giving him a stroke a hole.

2 **29 January 1791**
Mr Hamilton bets Mr Ferrier one gallon of claret that he beats him in 3 rounds playing with iron clubs.

3 **10 November 1821**
Mr Black Sen. lays £1 against Mr Finlayson. Mr Black playing with an iron club and receiving a half stroke each hole.

4 **14 December 1822**
Mr Black Sen. bets Mr Lindsay a gallon playing a putter and a heavy iron against Lindsay with all his clubs.

5 **26 June 1813**
Mr Laing offers a bet of a gallon that he will drive a ball 500 feet, giving him a chance of 10 strokes to accomplish it, and the choice of grounds.
(This shows that the feathery ball was capable of being hit over 150 yards. See p. 57.)

6 **16 April 1825**
James Stein v. Sim. Playing him with one hand and getting one stroke each hole. Lost by Mr Sim.

7 **26 April 1824**
Mr Black offers to play Mr Hastie one round, with a quart bottle, to tee his ball every stroke behind where it may lie and to have two strokes for one. Lost by Mr Hastie.

The results of such matches were not always recorded.

The Assembly Rooms

Returning to the Assembly Rooms after golf, the Captain always acted as Chairman for the dinner, a Deputy or 'Screw' (corkscrew) having been appointed for the occasion at the previous meeting. If the Captain could not turn up, his Deputy took his place or, if he was not there, the members selected one of their number. There was a fine of a gallon of claret for non-attendance of the 'Screw' without good reason. The business of the day was first attended to, including the ballotting for and admission of new members.

It was the custom among members often to present the Club

with a main dish–the favourite being a turtle. These were a great delicacy and they came from the connections the members appear to have had with the West Indies. Many turtles were presented over the years and the bill at the end of the season for dressing them was often quite substantial. On one occasion they had to buy one (7 August 1791)–it cost no less than £11–presumably dressed. Venison, geese and game were also given and everything was duly acknowledged in the minutes, including the shortage of grouse in 1834. In 1831 (23 July) the turtle given by Dr Boxall's brother was so large that 14 members and 14 guests fed off it and sufficient remained 'for a similar treat next Saturday'.*

The main drink was claret, and the standard measure for a fine was a gallon or Joram, value £1. Madeira is mentioned, and there were a number of gifts of champagne. The following entry is interesting;

> **'24 April 1824**
> Mr Robertson challenges Mr Black Sen. for a gallon of WHISKY. Mr Black giving Mr Robinson two strokes a hole which Mr R accepts solely for the good of the Club on account of it being for whisky.'

It is the first time whisky is mentioned which was subsequently to gain in popularity.

The toasts were numerous. Firstly there was the unwritten custom that a marriage or birth of a child merited a 'fine' of at least a gallon and examples have already been given (see pages 37–8). It appears that there was a list of Standing Toasts which became the subject of argument as new ones were suggested. On 19 January 1793 Mr Adam and Mr Barnes having interrupted the company a considerable time in disputing about toasts, the Chairman was pleased to fine them a gallon of claret each. On 1 November 1817 Mr Walker proposed that the 'Cricketers of England' be added to the list of Golf Club toasts but on the motion of Mr Longlands it was deferred until the following season and not heard of again. All sorts of toasts were proposed in both Clubs. The standing toasts of the Winter Club in November 1830 was limited to:

> Mother of Golfers
> The King or Queen
> The Hole the Baas and the Putter
> Stiff Shafts and Hard Baas (balls)

The toasts to the health of officers of the Club were curbed, the object being to preserve the harmony of the Club. It would appear that once the Standing Toasts had been drunk, the

* Turtles were shipped alive to England.
A recipe taken from Alexandre Dumas' *Dictionary of Cuisine* reads as follows and explains why the dressing of a turtle was expensive.

> 'To Prepare the Turtle. Tie your turtle to a ladder, head down. Attach a 60-pound weight to the neck, cut off the head, and let it bleed for 5 or 6 hours. Then lay it on its back on a table, detach the plastron, remove the intestines, cut off the fins, and collect the fat very carefully because of its delicacy. Cut the plastron and the carapace into 4 to 6 pieces, put them into a large cauldron of boiling water, and cook from 20 to 25 minutes, until the skin separates from the bones. Then take each piece and plunge it into cold water. Drain. The pieces of meat you will have taken out of the cauldron are not very delicate. They will be stringy and tasteless. The larger pieces are like veal rump. They can be larded and served as such provided you prepare them so as to heighten the flavour. In the culinary art everything is possible.'

Another recipe states that the shell of a turtle can be used as a dish and that a turtle weighing 120–180 lbs would serve fifty persons.

company proceeded to add to them, and having by that time consumed a fair quantity of claret, arguments then broke out. Here are one or two of the many other toasts:

1815
A satisfactory stroke to every golfer

12 September 1835
May we nair want baas when we most need them

1836
The Field Marshal–a fructifying wife to him

When they did have a good evening, they said so. August 1832: 'A most harmonious evening, dinner abundant, wines, food and conversation vastly superior and entertaining . . .' a toast given 'three times three' frequently occurs, going back to its earliest records–and it is a standard masonic toast.

All the visitors are recorded, and there are a number–particularly on the Anniversary Day when ladies were invited and some big parties were given–well organised with printed invitations, the accounts for which are still there. Among the more interesting visitors was Frederick, Duke of Brunswick-Wolfenbüttel, nephew of George III and brother to Caroline, the ill-used wife of the Prince Regent, who in the course of her troubled life lived at a house overlooking the Heath. The Duke was a popular visitor at the Anniversary Day celebrations in 1813 and 1814, and was then killed at the Battle of Quatre Bras two days before Waterloo in 1815. Among his staff was Col Nordenfelt, already referred to, who became an Honorary Member of the Knuckle Club.

Of the many other visitors, a close link was kept not only with Scots from Scotland but with visitors from overseas, and in 1831 the first link was forged with golf in India (see p. 75).

The period from 1830 to the early 1840s was one of slow decline for both Clubs in membership terms. There are however two interesting characters who by taking up residence at Blackheath over this period must have done a great deal to hold the Club together.

Captain Peter Cameron
(1777–1843)

Captain Cameron retired from the Honourable East India Company's Maritime Service circa 1829. He was a bachelor who formed a close friendship with Samuel Granger a master lighterman of Blackheath, also retired. Granger was a married man with no children. The two friends had joined forces and previously lived at 3 South Row, Blackheath, before Captain Cameron purchased No. 6 Eliot Place.

Captain Cameron was elected a member of the R.B.G.C. on 27

6 Eliot Place, Blackheath

June 1829 and Granger a month later on 11 July. Captain Cameron's house faced directly onto the old course and you could see the players from its window across Marr's Ravine, one of the principal hazards of those days but long since filled in. On 2 July 1831 Captain Cameron offered to contribute 100 guineas should Capt. Dobie obtain a Royal charter for the Club, and his health was drunk with high honours for his splendid offer but nothing more is heard of a Royal charter or patronage for many years.

Fittingly Capt. Cameron became Captain of the Club in April 1837 and Mr Granger was installed a year later to succeed him. Capt. Cameron was a Scot from Inverness and went to Aberdeen University before joining the East India Company's service in 1799 and must have learnt his golf there and it looks as though he persuaded Samuel Granger to take up the game. Their residence, 6 Eliot Place, still stands overlooking the Heath which has totally changed in appearance.

Finally a word about the membership of the Blackheath Clubs which, throughout this period, remained almost exclusively Scottish. There were new arrivals from Scotland and departures of those returning to live in Scotland. There were those who left to join the East India Company or who retired from it and membership links with India, the Far East and the West Indies.

The Army and Navy from Woolwich and Greenwich and other members of the Services were always welcome. Like the Scottish Clubs they had their problems with members who failed to pay their subscriptions but on the other hand the Clubs (Summer and Winter), even in the lean years of the 1830s, were never in financial difficulty. At the turn of the nineteenth century they received several legacies and accumulated a capital fund of some £700–a substantial sum in those days.

The end of the Summer and Winter Clubs came quite suddenly, in 1843, and no explanation or reasons were given. We have examined the minutes of the two Clubs from 1825–1843 to see if we could find any justification for having two Clubs with separate membership, both using the Green Man and the same golf course. It has been pointed out to us that whilst masonic qualifications for Golfing Societies were relaxed, there was nothing to prevent the retention of masonic control through the recruitment of new members who were already masons. They also both kept up the traditional dining routine. Whatever the explanation, new members were not coming in.

It was moved on 11 June 1834 that 'it is due to the character of the Golf Club that their meetings at the Green Man should cease so soon as arrangements for a removal can be perfected'. They did not move but a minute of 20 August 1836 reads: 'The Cream of the Club met today–only Captain Kemp and Secretary Masson, and on 3 September 1836 "Few but select, dinner good, game absent without leave".' Whatever the explanation, a new course, a new Blackheath Club, a new Clubhouse and a relaxed dinner commitment had a dramatic effect, as we shall see.

Marr's Ravine. Published by D. Walther, Brydges Street, Covent Garden, London 1823 (by permission of the Guildhall Library)

Chapter 4 The heyday of Blackheath (1843–1920)

The Winter Golf Club was dissolved in 1844. Mr John Masson resigned–he had been Registrar for 17 years and Secretary of Blackheath Golf Club for 12 years. The original Medal of The Knuckle had been transferred to the Blackheath Golf Club and was the Spring Medal of that Club. The Club extended its season to the whole year, the first day of the year being 1st April.

The course was altered, the number of holes was increased from 5 to 7 and, more importantly, the holes now frequently crossed the gravel pits instead of skirting them. New regulations and new rules of the game were drawn up and approved. Most of this activity was dealt with by Major H. Jelf Sharp, Honorary Secretary and Treasurer. Shortly after the Club took over, as a temporary lease, a house at No. 3 College Place, Maidenstone Hill. Between 1844 and 1854 the membership rose sharply.

The impression is of a Golf Club becoming an open and active Club in which the playing of golf was becoming more important than the dining. As a result the members made themselves a larger, more difficult and challenging golf course. Golf was King of the Heath. They sought a final solution to the Clubhouse problem, a Clubhouse which was to provide shelter and changing accommodation for the gentlemen golfers rather than a roof under which they could over-indulge in food and drink, using golf as a means of shaking up their livers and promoting both appetite and thirst.

They demonstrated the emphasis on golf by reducing the dinner meetings from 12 annually to 7 in 1844 and subsequently from 7 to 4 in 1879: at this time dinners were only held on the major Medal Days. It is also noticeable, at this time, that bets on non-golfing matters became markedly fewer: there were more bets made at the dinners on golf and the bets themselves changed. Gallons of claret were fewer and more modest bets of money became the general rule.

They further emphasised their intention to concentrate on playing golf well by appointing an eminent and famous golf professiontal from Scotland in 1851–Willie Dunn Senior–and three years later his twin brother, James, as well.

As the interest of members in golf and golfing prowess continued, so they acquired more trophies for which to play. In 1844 there were two scratch golf Medals–the Spring (the old Knuckle Club) Medal and the Summer Medal. By 1890 they had three more–The Bombay Silver Medal, The Golf Medal of the Blackheath Photographic Society and the George Glennie Gold Medal. In addition they had been given, or had acquired for

Willie and Jamie Dunn

themselves, five Silver Cups, the Calcutta, the Singapore, the Penn, the Knill and the Adam. All the trophies were played for annually, the medals being for scratch competition and the silver cups for handicap competition.

An additional factor which promoted golf on the Heath was the advent of the railway which considerably improved access from London.

In 1836 the first railway service to Greenwich was opened; this revolutionised local travel between South-East London and the City. It was followed in July 1849 by the opening of the North Kent branch of the South-Eastern Railway, from London Bridge to Lewisham, Blackheath, Charlton and Woolwich, a half-hourly service taking only twenty minutes. The Blackheath fare was 1s, 1st class, 9d, 2nd, and 6d, 3rd class. The service from Charing Cross followed in 1864. There was an ample service of cabs to the Golf Clubhouse, the fare being 1s 6d.

A pleasant, unwritten, rule of the Club, after the arrival of the railway, was that on each Club day, excepting those days upon which a competition was held, every member appearing at the Clubhouse by a stated time, (varying with the season of the year and fixed by the Committee, having regard to the arrivals of the train from Town) could be sure of having a match.

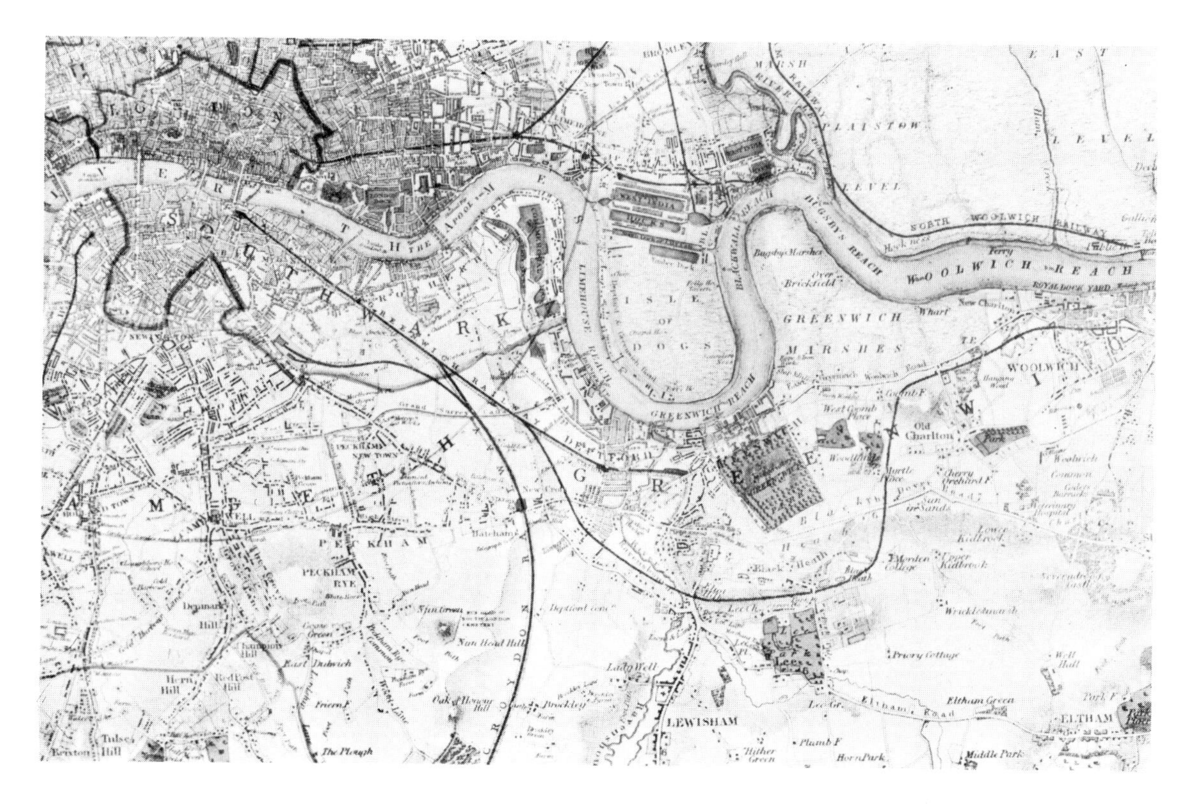

Map of South East London area *c.* 1860, showing Greenwich Railway

What of the Blackheath course from 1844? This was the 7-hole course of which a plan exists and was designed with some care, not, as apparently the earlier 5-hole course was designed, to be played between the gravel pits and avoiding the roads, but using the gravel pits and roads as hazards. This course is sometimes referred to as the Hazard Course.

At the first hole, 170 yards, play was across a local road and a portion of the Old Gravel Pit. The green was close to the far edge of the pit and behind it was the main London/Dover Road. The 2nd tee was near the first green, close to the road, and went across another portion of the pit, then across a road to the green, on the left of which was another gravel pit, known as Marr's Ravine. On the right of the green was another road. Length 335 yards. The 3rd-hole (380 yards) tee was on the edge of Marr's Ravine and the player was required to drive over the Ravine, across two roads and then to a green which was immediately across the main Dover Road and had on its right side one of the minor roads crossing the Heath and on its left side yet another old gravel pit. The 4th-hole (540 yards) tee was near the 3rd green: this very long hole crossed Shooters Hill Road and there was a large gravel pit which had to be carried, or circumvented, before the green was reached, this being situated in a corner made by the junction of Charlton Road and a road crossing the Heath, now known as Prince Charles Road.

London from Greenwich Park engraved by T. A. Prior. Published by J. & W. Robins 1840 (by permission of the Guildhall Library)

The 5th hole (500 yards) came back in the opposite direction and crossed a large old gravel pit and Shooters Hill Road before the green was to be found, immediately on the other side of the Dover Road; behind the green was one of the minor Heath roads. The 6th hole (230 yards) a two-shotter, started by the 5th green. The green was guarded in front and on the right by a Heath road passing Heath House and Mill House and was in a triangle between the gardens of Heath House and Mill House on the left, a road behind the green and by the Heath road already mentioned. The 7th-hole (410 yards) tee was a little way from the 6th green; from the tee, a Heath road had to be crossed (later known as Golfers Road) and then another perilous shot across the old gravel pit which featured in the 1st and 2nd holes, to a green guarded in front by the old Whitefield Road and on the right by another road. The congestion and general danger at this gravel pit must have been of a high order but was no doubt made somewhat safer by the presence of caddies and of forecaddies also, the latter armed with red flags to warn the general public on the Heath of the presence of golfers.

The roads across the Heath were mostly one or two feet below the level of the Heath, and, although not metalled roads, would certainly have been stony. They must have constituted very difficult hazards, especially as many of them were quite close to the green, necessitating a delicate stroke rather than a full swing. It goes without saying that the gravel pits, as shown in the picture on p. 52 of Marr's Ravine, were very formidable hazards indeed. See also Chapter 3, p. 60. We are told in the *Chronicles* that the course was very rough in its early days, with deep hollows in the pits, steep banks sloping down and many whins and bushes. Over the years whins were uprooted or burnt, the deep hollows gradually filled in, and, no doubt, many pebbles and stones removed from the 'fairways'. Never-the-less, Bernard Darwin wrote, in 1910, of F. S. Ireland, that he had an uncanny ability to tear the ball out of the flinty Blackheath lies.

Seven holes may seem a curious number today but 7-hole courses were common in Scotland in the early days of golf. The usual 'round' was 21 holes on the Hazard Course. On the earlier, 5-hole, course a 'round' had been 15 holes. To a present-day golfer the full difficulties of this course, apart from the fact that it was rough and full of pits and bad lies, may not be apparent. The 7-hole course was 2,565 yards long. This is the equivalent to an 18-hole course of approximately 6,174 yards and three rounds of 7 holes, the usual competition round, would have represented 7,095 yards. Today 18 holes of 6,174 yards is a short course, but when one considers the crude clubs in use and the feathery or gutta golf balls this must have been a very long course indeed. In 1813, as mentioned in Chapter 3 Mr Charles Laing made a bet that he would drive a ball 500 feet, being allowed 10 shots in which to do it. This represents 166 yards. Mr Laing is recorded as being a winner of both the Silver Club and the Medal of the Knuckle Club, so he must be considered a good golfer in his day. This makes a 330-yard hole a very long two-shotter and holes of 500 and 540 yards a 'par' 6, even for expert golfers.

On numerous occasions play did not take place because the day was 'too boisterous' and there is little doubt that Blackheath was a windy heath–hence no doubt the presence of a number of windmills. Putting was difficult, as the greens were not much more than a patch of fairway with short grass, as is shown in the 'Golfing Group'–showing George Glennie putting. When Willie Park Jnr wrote the first definitive book on putting, *The Art of Putting* (1920), he describes methods of putting out of a poor lie which gives some indication of the roughness of greens on most courses at that time: he was referring to greens prior to 1900.

The Club Staff

One suspects that the Blackheath course was difficult and, not only that, but was in poor condition, which made it even more difficult. The members spared no effort to rectify the problems of course condition and devised a unique system of greenkeeping staff to deal with it. This system has been mentioned briefly (see p.45). Payments were made to the Greenwich men (Royal Naval Hospital Pensioners from Greenwich) of 1s on Medal Days; each man was assigned a hole to look after–so there were seven in all on the Hazard Course–his job being to look after the 'green' (meaning the entire hole) and the flag. These men were solely concerned with the course and were additional to the caddies and forecaddies (also Greenwich, or 'College', men) which all players would have had.

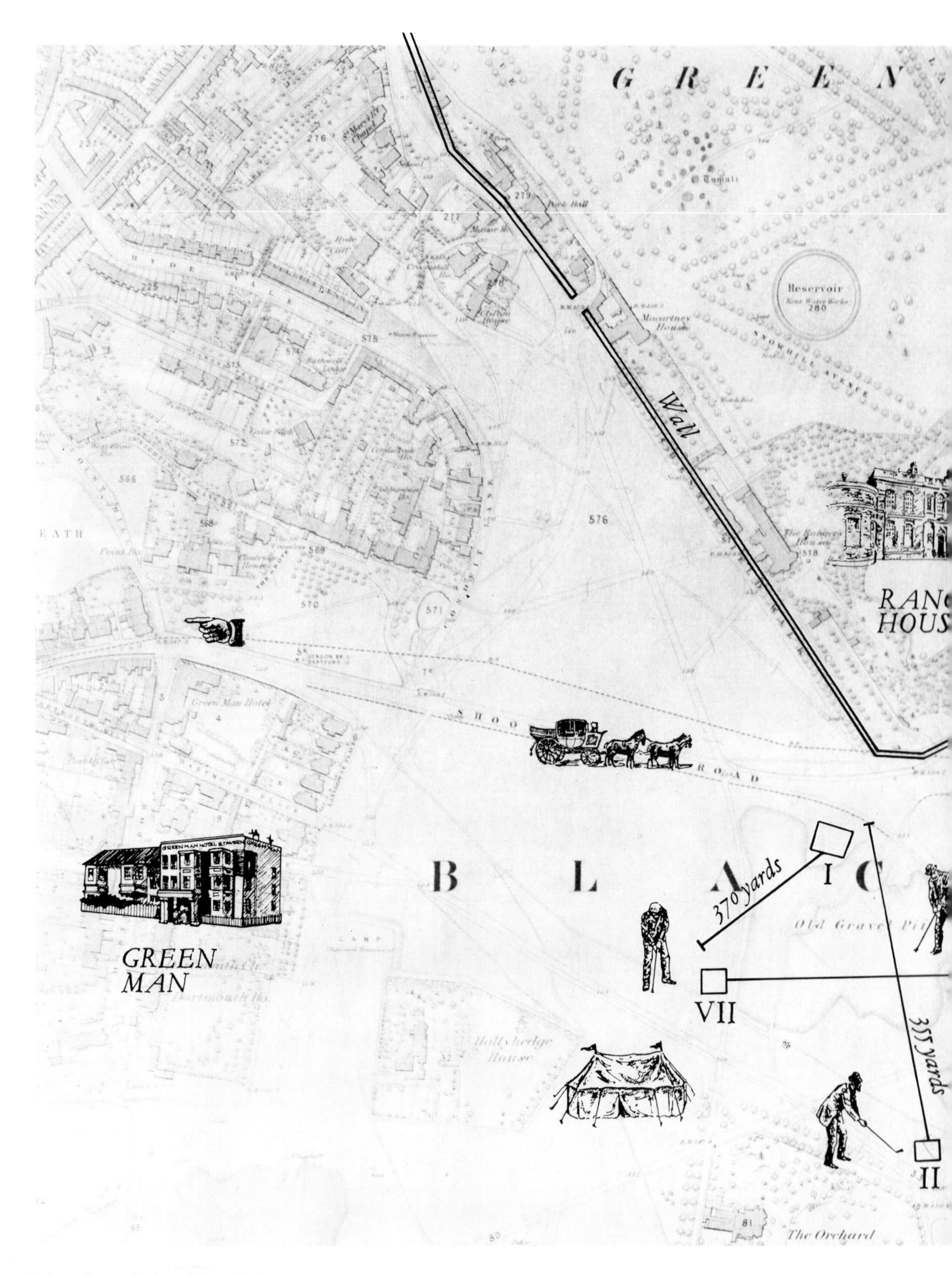

Map of the 7-hole or Hazard Course

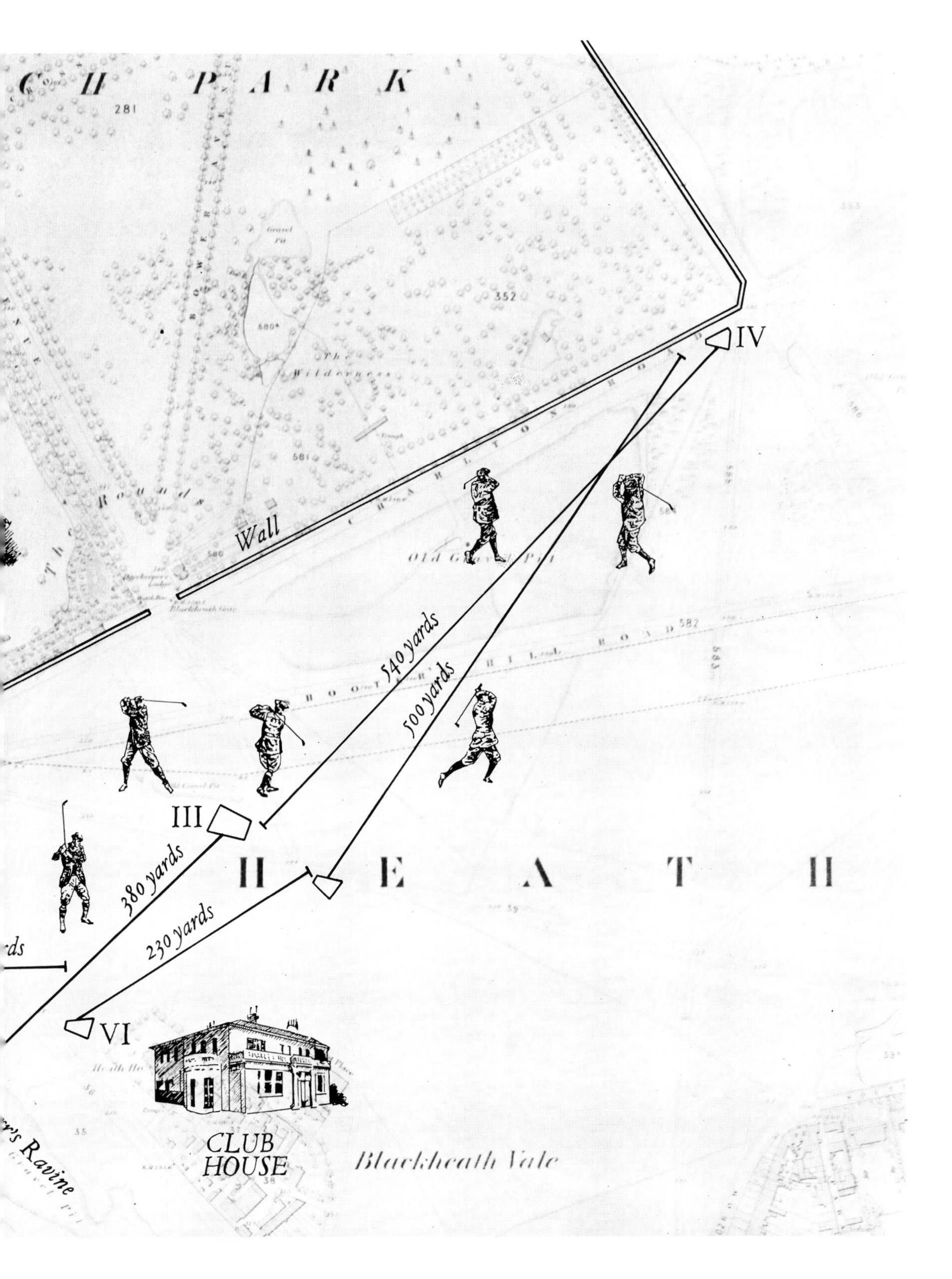

P A R K
Wall
IV
III
VI
540 yards
500 yards
380 yards
230 yards
H E A T H
CLUB HOUSE
Blackheath Vale
Old Gravel Pit
The Wilderness

Marr's Ravine, *c.* 1920

Unfortunately, the Greenwich Hospital closed its doors in 1869, so that these picturesque additions to the golfing scene disappeared; but the custom of one man to look after each hole continued until about 1900.

That there was continued effort to improve the course is shown in a minute of March 1878: 'The Putting Greens being in a very unsatisfactory state for a considerable time it was thought to form a Greens Committee'. Eventually, one member, Mr William McCandlish, a civil engineer who lived on the edge of the Heath, was deputed to be responsible for the greens. This may well be one of the first recorded attempts to constitute a Greens Committee.

The Holemakers

Blackheath seems to be unique in having, specifically, men to cut holes. This job does not appear to have warranted a specialist on seaside links, where, in the sandy soil, any artisan could cut a hole with a knife using a galley pot for size, or could use a holecutter, an instrument which is known to have existed from 1829 in Scotland. At Westward Ho! in 1864 it was customary for the first competitor to go off in the Medal to cut the holes with a clasp knife and, often, to mark the position, by sticking a gull's feather in the ground. Blackheath almost certainly needed this specialist because of the difficulty of cutting holes in stony, gravelly, ground, which must have needed some skill and patience. In the

Portion of Blackheath Common today

earlier times the clubmaker was also the holecutter, e.g. a minute of 7 November 1807, in which it is stated that Donaldson's bill for holemaking, amounting to £3 6s 0d is to be paid–he is also listed as a clubmaker. On many occasions the records report that the holemaker was paid a sum but give no name. Clubmakers usually were given a name and were more important men. 'Old Alick', a caddy who became a holemaker in about 1822, as well, was probably the best known and remembered of all the holemakers and his portrait hangs in the Clubhouse (see illustration on p. 19).

The Clubmakers and Professionals

It should be realised that in the nineteenth century, in Scotland, there was a Club servant known as the 'Keeper of the Green'. The term 'Green' meant golf links or course. This man had charge of the course or links and was responsible to the Club Secretary. He was in charge of those who worked on the course and had a knowledge of how to look after greens and bunkers; he was also in charge of the caddies and of those caddies who occasionally played golf with the members by reason of having an extra skill at the game–the professionals. The Keeper of the Green also had a workshop and was skilled at making and repairing golf clubs. The caddie was the lowest rung in the ladder, and the 'professional', who caddied when he could not get a game and often had a second job for the winter when there was little golf, was but little higher in status than the caddie. It seems that at Blackheath there was no Keeper of the Green but there was a clubmaker, who, from his salary, was the most senior of the Club servants on the course and almost certainly had control over the holecutter and the College men assigned to each hole on Medal Days.

As was common in those days, the servant class were not long lived.

Donaldson, clubmaker, appears on the books in 1787, being paid 10 guineas for clubmaking. In 1806 he has a 'severe accident' and is voted 1½ guineas a week for 3 weeks; in 1815 the Club pays for his funeral.

Ballantyne followed him, in the winter of 1815. What happened to him we do not know, but we next have:

Cockburn in April 1817. In 1820 he was in a bad state of health. He was to be paid 'the usual 6s a week in the Winter' and an additional shilling because of his health. In 1822 he had an 'Assistant Holemaker'. Later in 1822 he received his allowance and immediately after the Club paid for his funeral.

Poke and *Beetson* 1823, both clubmakers. Poke obviously the senior (and better paid), possibly Beetson was his assistant/apprentice, but, late in 1823:

Sharpe 'Mr. Black propos'd Archd Sharpe to be clubmaker in future': 3/6 per week was allowed as a salary. (See portrait on p. 24). In 1830 Sharpe's coat and waistcoat were paid for, possibly he was given a Club uniform but this is not stated. In 1832 the Club buys Sharpe a new suit of clothes. In 1829, £2 17s was paid, being the Surgeon's bill for Sharpe. In 1834, the death of poor Sharpe is recorded, together with the thanks of the Club to Dr Ferrier, a member of the Club who looked after him in his last illness; the Secretary was to order 'a decent and economic funeral'. The cost was £7; clearly the Club looked after its servants and, as further evidence of this, in 1834, when Sharpe was dying, he wrote a letter to the Club expressing great relief that the Club had used its influence to get his son admitted into the Caledonian Asylum.

There is little to indicate the presence of a clubmaker after this and it is possible that the Club being in a poor way and with few members there was not enough money or work to employ one. It seems that at about this time or perhaps later, in association with Dunn, there were other artisans in the ball- and clubmaking craft, who are not recorded. In a document relating to the lease of the Clubhouse of 1869–1889 (93, Blackheath Hill) from Morden College, it is noted that the house had previously been occupied by Archibald Hamilton David Henry and Alexander Duncan Anderson, now deceased, club- and ballmakers.

The Dunns. With the new 7-hole Hazard Course and a rising membership, Willie Dunn from North Berwick was appointed in 1851. He was both a skilled clubmaker and a considerable golfer. One could therefore say that he was the first Blackheath professional in the meaning of the modern term. The bringing of a well-known (and presumably well paid) professional from Scotland was an important step; it may well have been connected with the advent of the gutta percha ball in Blackheath three years previously and the fact that Sir Thomas Moncrieffe (Captain of Blackheath 1854) had sent some sheet gutta percha to Willie Dunn at North Berwick at that time (see Chapter 9). The Dunns were men of enterprise and Willie may well have perceived the importance of this new discovery and decided to move nearer the source of supply. James Dunn, his twin brother, joined him at Blackheath about two years later.

Willie was married and his two sons Tom, later to be professional and clubmaker at Royal Wimbledon, and Willie Jnr, later to be professional at Westward Ho! and, later still, to be a leading professional and golf architect in America, were both born at Blackheath. In 1864 the Dunns got into trouble at the Club (and this included Mrs Dunn as well). Alcohol appears to have played a part and there were subsequent summonses to appear before the Secretary, complaints of rudeness, demands for apology, etc. By 1865 the Dunns had gone back to Leith.

It is curious and interesting that when the first 'open' Championship was played in 1860 there were only eight contestants, one of whom was George Daniel Brown of Blackheath. This 'open' was not really open because it was confined to Scotland only. George Daniel Brown was allowed to play only because Blackheath made a particular request that their Club be included (see *Story of the Open Golf Championship*, p. 26). The Dunns, who were both well-known golfers, did not enter. G. D. Brown was fifth (out of eight) with a score of 192. George Daniel Brown is listed in Slater's Trade Directory as clubmaker of St Andrews in 1867. How he came to play for Blackheath is not known: possibly he was an apprentice in the Dunns' workshop.

Charles Hunter, 1866. This man, an apprentice of the great Tom Morris at Prestwick (of which town Hunter was a native), appears in the Blackheath records on 20 May 1865 when he was paid £4 16s for his expenses to the interview at Blackheath. He started in 1866 at 17s 6d a week for the first six months and 1 guinea (21s) a week for the second six months. The Club were a little cautious and, as it turned out, rightly, for on the death of Strath, the then professional at Prestwick in 1868, Hunter applied for his job, got it, and returned to his native town where he remained until his death many years later.

Robert Kirk. Appointed professional and clubmaker in about 1868. A St Andrews man who was a good golfer and a good clubmaker. His salary at the time of his appointment was 15s a week, but, by 1870, he complained to the Committee that on his salary he could not pay his way, and his salary was raised to 20s a week. In 1872 he was paid £78 p.a. and this rose to £79 in 1879 and to £104 in 1880. He had other sources of income as well. The second scratch prize in many of the competitions was 'golf clubs' and many records of results mention this. The handicap winner received golf balls. Kirk was paid for both clubs and gutta balls which he, no doubt, made e.g. on 3 March 1873: 'Prize clubs and Balls £3 1s 6d'. Kirk was also paid on Competition Days for organising the flagmen, etc.: '1869 Flagmen and Robt Kirk 1s 2d'. 1871 'Flagmen and allowance to Robt Kirk 19s.' Kirk was not discouraged from playing at other Clubs at Blackheath's expense, e.g. in 1872 Royal Liverpool asked permission for Robert Kirk to attend the Golf Tournament there in the Spring. The Committee agreed. In 1873 Kirk was given permission by the Committee to attend a Golf Meeting at Westward Ho!. In 1873, 'Allowance to Kirk to two days at Dartford Heath £1', 'Paid R. Kirk one day at Wimbledon 10/–'.

He seems, nevertheless, to have had occasional troubles; and in 1873 Mr William Noakes complained to the Committee of Kirk's rudeness: Kirk apologised. In 1874 R. Kirk was paid £1 10s for making an ebony club. Some time in 1876 he left and was succeeded by Thomas Manzie. In 1885 Tom Morris, writing from St Andrews, recommended C. Thomson as Manzie's successor. He, in turn, was succeeded by George Brews in 1890. Brews was followed by T. Castle, but Castle died in 1906. The duties of Castle's successor were to be:

> Supervision of the Greens
> Handing out of flags and clubs
> Paying the caddies
> Keeping all clubs left in the shop clean and to carry out all the duties which a professional is normally expected to do.

His wages were to be £1 2s 6d a week. Blackheath continued the tradition, starting with Donaldson in 1797, of obtaining their professionals from Scotland, at least until 1900. They allowed their professionals to concentrate on golf and clubs, having other Club servants to attend to the upkeep of the course, such as holecutters and other greens' staff, e.g. 1899 £52 paid to

A portion of the picture 'Golf at Blackheath', 1875. In the foreground is Robert Kirk, Professional at Blackheath 1868–1876 (see pp. 20–21)

Tomlinson 'for the putting greens' and in 1902 £55 to Brett for the same purpose. They did not discourage their professionals, after 1870, from playing on other courses.

Clubhouses and Club Stewards

In 1843 Blackheath acquired No. 3 College Place, Royal Hill, as a temporary Clubhouse for six months at a rental of £15 for the half year. Robert Brand was employed as a Club servant; he was to be capable of making and mending clubs and taking charge of members' boxes; in 1845, then of 3 Maidenstone Terrace, he had been employed as a clubmaker and was the ratepayer at No. 3 College Hill before the Club took it over. A suitable room was to be provided for members to change their dress and have access to their boxes throughout the year. This was all to be provided at an annual expense not exceeding £30. Brand may be considered more of a Club Steward than a clubmaker because when Willie Dunn was appointed in 1851 both he and Brand were employed at 15s a week. Clearly, Dunn, who was a highly skilled man, was going to deal with clubs and it must be assumed either that there was too much work for Brand to do both jobs or, that Brand was not particularly good at clubmaking and repairing and that the Club, in pursuing its policy of improving the golf, appointed a proper expert who could, moreover, give instruction in the art of playing the game.

One can well imagine that the Steward had plenty to do. Although the Clubhouse was not used often as a dining place but as a place where members could change and keep their boxes, he would have been busy keeping things clean and tidy, cleaning shoes etc. and additionally he would be responsible for erecting the tent on Medal Days. While Brand had plenty to do, the Club also employed other servants to look after things.

There were stewardesses or housekeepers (history does not give them a title) who clearly played an important part in the running of the Clubhouse. The first of these ladies was Mrs Reynolds in about 1855; she was paid the same salary as Willie Dunn, so she must have been a fairly important Club servant. Her duties (and those of her successors Mrs Dryborough and Mrs Hill) are not specified but throughout the accounts 'Mrs. Reynolds Book a/c' has to be met each month. Another Club servant who is mentioned in the accounts with some regularity is 'Moses' who looked after the Clubhouse garden.

The members' boxes were long narrow boxes in which were kept, primarily, members' clubs and, no doubt, also some spare shoes and garments. They were the forerunner of golf lockers and also, to a certain extent, of golf bags for, although not carried on the course, it was customary to carry golf clubs in them when travelling. The professionals in the latter half of the nineteenth century, when called upon to travel to tournaments or give exhibitions, usually took their golf boxes with them. Golf boxes were usually not fixed, like lockers in a later time, and were often laid flat on the floor of the changing room and had a handle for carrying them.

The following account of a medal at Blackheath in 1874 is reprinted in full because it is one of the few contemporary accounts of a day's golf and because it seems fair to describe the game and its players at that time.

'A Medal Day at Blackheath'

Tis an ill wind that blows nobody good. The grey skies and east winds of yesterday were bad for Ascot; but they were appropriate enough over the bleak and sandy undulations of Blackheath, where the golfers had come to compete for their summer medal. Many of the hardy Scotchmen who came out in their scarlet jackets and white breeches must have fancied they were at home again–that they were playing on the famous links of St. Andrews, or by the Fair City of Perth, or within sight of Salisbury Crags. Might they not, with a little imagination, have

Key to 'Golf at Blackheath' (see pp. 20–21)

changed the scene, taking the distant slopes of Shooter's-hill for a sort of reduced Arthur's Seat, the windings of the Thames at Greenwich for the windings of the Forth, and recognising all around that prevailing mist that comes in from the sea to tone down the colours of Scotland's capital? But perhaps in the excitement of "teeing" they

> Forgot the clouded Forth,
> The gloom that saddens Heaven and Earth,
> The bitter east, and misty summer,
> And grey metropolis of the North,

and proceeded with their accustomed ardour to show their southern rivals how to go safely and boldly round a "course." It was possible, indeed, in many cases to apportion the nationality of the combatants, even though no explanatory music heralded their approach.

Here, for example, are two players who have just come on to the green plain of the Heath from the Dover road–that Dover road on which, we have been informed by good authority, mile-stones are to be found. One is a man of sixty-five or so, six feet in height, broad-shouldered, with a majestic white beard and keen grey eyes looking out from under shaggy eyebrows. Those eyes, one may well imagine, have watched for the first appearance of the red deer as dawn broke over the mists of the Jura mountains, and then woe to the first stag that came along the rocks in advance of the herd! In addition to the scarlet jacket, and instead of the orthodox white trousers, he wears rough and serviceable knickerbockers: they may have brushed the heather on the moorlands of Ross or in the moist valleys of the far island of Lewis. The other is a handsome young man of a thoroughly English type, slender in make and soft in feature, with fair hair, light grey eyes, and sun-tanned face. They are preceded by a scout, who carries a red flag. The scout is not a tall and stalwart gillie in kilts, but a short, stout, in-kneed youth, who seems to have just left his barrow round the corner, and who would probably prove an ugly customer in a rush along the Strand on a Lord Mayor's Day. They are attended by two other persons, also apparently costermongers out of work, each of whom carries an armful of the implements used in the game, and who is supposed to hand the necessary club, spoon, or putter when his master requires it. There are few people on the Heath. The spectators are chiefly boys, who take their position at critical points, and soon get to acquire a sufficient knowledge of this occult game to calculate the chances of the players, although they might not be able to estimate accurately the value of "one off three." For the rest, there is little picturesqueness about the scene–except for these bits of scarlet colour scattered over the dull green of the Heath. It is a sombre day. The houses and trees about shut out the grey river and its masts. Shooter's-hill looks distant in the thin fog; there is not a break in the low-toned sky; and the gallant golfer is not the less inclined to consider himself back in Scotland again when he overhears his companion suddenly say to a dilatory attendant, "Whut the deevil ur ye daein' here? Get on, man!" It is thus that they sing the songs of Zion in a strange land.

Now at the beginning of the game a little law is allowed; and if the player chooses he may place the small white ball on a tiny heap of sand in order to deliver the first blow more effectually. Shall we calculate the chances of the new comers by this "teeing"? MacCallum-Mhor, having carefully placed the ball, kicks aside a twig here or there to clear the way, grasps his club, straightens up his shoulders, and has a look across the broad and shallow sand-pit near him, on the farther side of which stands the scout with his red flag. Up goes the club over his shoulder, there is a moment's deliberation, and then the rapid blow is delivered–sending the ball whistling through the air some hundred and fifty yards or so before it drops, while we see it thereafter go bounding on to within a dozen yards of the red flag. The younger man also carefully places his ball; he too measures his distance, and delivers a heavy blow–but, somehow, the ball flies off at an angle, it drops short of the opposite crest, and comes rolling down into the hollow. By the time the small crowd of people has walked round to the other side of this little valley, the players have already crossed, and each is doing his utmost to get his ball, with the fewest possible number of strokes, into a certain small hole dug in the ground. But then MacCallum-Mhor has it all his own way; for at the very first stroke he came within a few yards of this particular spot. At present his ball is within three-quarters of a yard of the small black hole. He chooses a particular club; measures distance and direction carefully; gives the ball a tap, and as straight as a line can go it trundles along and disappears. He picks it out; tosses it to an attendant to be sponged; and takes another to continue the game. If there were any betting going on, the small crowd would be inclined to back the elder of these two players.

And what it the opinion which the unexcited Southron forms of this imported pastime? Well, it is obviously one that involves a good deal of physical effort, as well as the exercise of trained skill of various kinds. In the case of long courses, the holes or goals are sometimes a quarter of a mile apart; and a good player must be prepared to put all his strength into the blow which he then deals at the ball. Then he must be able to judge distances accurately; he must be capable of taking sure aim and sending the ball in a straight line; and he must have experience of the various chances which may befall him on uneven ground. The golf-player does not desire a smooth plain. His best ground lies near the sea, where the sand has been washed in bygone ages into all sorts of gentle hills and dales; and failing that, an occasional gravel-pit offers the best obstruction he can get. When one of the longed-for holes lies close by the brink of some abrupt hollow, the manoeuvring with which a skilful player will get his ball over the hollow, and yet not too far on the other side, is beautiful to witness. There is not, certainly, the nicety of billiard playing in the performance; but there is a vast deal more of exercise in the game, and the air that one breathes–even when the east winds are blowing–is preferable to the gas-smoke of a billard-room. Indeed, there is so much exercise in the game that one can observe our hardy mountaineers who hail from the north puffing and blowing at times in a fashion which suggests that they are not quite in condition to go "chasing the wild deer and following the roe." Perhaps our southern fashions have corrupted them. City dinners are not a good preparation for work of this sort. The mountaineer's legs may keep firm enough, but heavy luncheons begin to alter his figure somewhat and keep him scant of breath. Ought the corpulent golfer to "Bant," or trust to his favourite exercie to restore to him his wonted

Medal Day at Blackheath from the *Daily News* of 1874

length of wind? The latter is the more natural method, certainly, although we are in these times so given over to the teachings of physiology that one can scarcely understand how Shakspeare managed to get through such an enormous amount of intellectual labour, considering that he was probably unaware of the fact that there is phosphorus in fish, and that Greek wines are good for the exhausted brain.

The Clubhouse at No. 93 Blackheath Hill (1865–1909). From a sketch by Pinkerton

(This was taken from the *Daily News* of June 1874 and reprinted in R. Clark's *Golf–A Royal and Ancient Game* (first published 1875 (together with the illustration)).

Comments on *A Medal Day at Blackheath*.

Although the commentator feels that the golfing scene is somewhat dull and colourless (owing no doubt to the misty day) the scene would have been far from colourless to today's golfers. Scarlet coats, white satin trousers, forecaddies with red flags and some red hats, the tent by the first tee and the flag flying in the breeze, lamp posts on the Heath, the Dover to London traffic passing by; groups of small boys in rags of clothes with bare feet or wearing clogs, running ahead around or through the gravel pits to see the next shot, or to find the ball in the bottom of the pit.

Match at Blackheath by F. Gilbert, 1869

These accompaniments to golf, together with the general bustle of the Heath and the silent windmills, conjure up a picture of colour and a sense of atmosphere which was (golfingly speaking) unique.

Clubhouse Moves

From its temporary house at College Place, Royal Hill, the Club moved in 1849 to No. 97, a house close to the top of Blackheath Hill and, from here they moved to a house slightly lower down the hill (No. 93) and this became the permanent Clubhouse in 1865 and remained so until 6 July 1909 when they took over Heath House, close to the 6th green (see map). To this house they moved all their treasures and it continued to be their Clubhouse until about 1924–5, when, the Club having merged with Eltham in 1923, Eltham taking over the title Royal Blackheath Golf Club, they finally moved all their treasures to the new Clubhouse, where they remain today. They nevertheless, kept the old Clubhouse on until 1951, using it as a social club, and for playing cards.

Golfing Prowess at Blackheath

We have seen the development of the Club from a dining club with some golf played and much dining and wining with a proportion of bets not concerning golf, to a predominantly Golfing Club, with fewer dinners, more modest bets and those on the golf. The discipline of the masonic tradition was carried on and resulted in a well-organised Club with strict rules–regular and well-attended competitions being played on a new course of 7 holes, to which was given care and attention for its continued improvement. The Club servants were numerous and club-makers and professionals were of the highest standard. Close attention was paid to the rules and regulations of the game, even to the extent of having markers to accompany each pair and scrutineers selected at the dinner to decide who had won. This improvement increased the number of members and the general keenness on golf as a result of which, in the 1860s and 1870s, Blackheath could boast a collection of fine golfers; medal scores steadily improved and Blackheath golfers could hold their own in any golfing company.

Detailed records of all scores are dull and unnecessary, but some general remarks and comparisons may be helpful. As has been said in Chapter 3 p.47 the scores on the old 5-hole course by 1820–40 were, roughly, averaging c.110 for the 15-hole round, an average of about 7.5 strokes per hole. The hazard Course was of 7 holes, 3 rounds (or 21 holes) constituting a round. If this course was the equal of the 5-hole course in difficulty one might expect medal scores of $7.5 \times 21 = 157.5$ strokes. The Hazard Course was, in fact, more difficult as you had to play across the gravel pits and both pits and local roads were deliberately arranged to make hazards near the greens. The first score in 1847 (by Hon. Fox Maule) was 175 but on this, one, occasion the Medal was played over 4 rounds i.e., 28 holes. Within a few years, scores of 130 were being recorded. Even allowing for the fact that the gutta ball had arrived, this improvement of about 27 shots in 21 holes is very impressive. By 1870–1880 scores of 120 were appearing–an improvement of a further 10 shots. By the end of the century F. S. Ireland had established a course record of 101 and a general run of scores around 112–114 were common. Clearly the standard of golf at Blackheath rose rapidly during the latter half of the nineteenth century but, although this local improvement occurred, did Blackheath measure up, in its standard of golf, to the recognised golfing giants of Scotland? It did and in 1857 they proved it.

A great Foursomes Tournament was arranged at St Andrews, the concept being first put forward by Prestwick Golf Club, at which seven leading Scots Clubs were invited–Blackheath was the eighth Club. George Glennie and Lieut J. C. Stewart sallied north to represent Blackheath and won! En route, they beat Royal Perth, Innerleven, Bruntsfield and, in the final, the R. & A.,

Pamphlet of the Great Tournament
1867

A Professional Golf Tournament at Blackheath *c.* 1890

by seven holes, no less. Thus Blackheath triumphantly proved their worth in Open Competition.

That the Blackheath course was difficult was shown when, toward the end of the nineteenth century, J. H. Taylor, then at the height of his powers, won a tournament at Blackheath with a score of 99 and expressed himself as well pleased to have been able to break 100.

Chapter 5 Blackheath as a promoter of golf

Cynics might say that Blackheath, in aiding golfers in England to form Golf Clubs, was merely promoting its own interest, so that they might play on other courses and compete against other Golf Clubs without having to travel all the way to Scotland. No doubt this would have crossed the minds of the members of Blackheath because, although much of the membership was of Scottish origin, most had been living in England for many years and were successful businessmen with many English acquaintances from other parts of England whom they had met in London.

The general impression one gets is of a genuine interest in promoting golf for purely altruistic reasons and nothing bears this out more than their interest in golf overseas. There seems to have been a fraternal feeling with those who golfed abroad, partly a remnant of freemasonry and partly because many were brother Scots earning their living abroad. Those who played abroad had a feeling for the Blackheath Golf Club; some may well have been members because, if you wanted to play golf outside Scotland before 1864, there were only two Clubs to which you could belong. Many of those abroad had been sent by London business houses. These individual people sent (or brought) presents back for the Club (*vide* all the turtles mentioned on p. 49) so that it was quite understandable, that when groups of such individuals abroad decided to form Golf Clubs, they not only informed Blackheath but sought their advice and help. Such advice and help was unfailingly provided by Blackheath. There were important and early associations with Clubs in India because of the large number of British people employed by the East India Company.

Calcutta Golf Club

The minutes of 12 June 1830 record the formation of a Club at Dum Dum (near Calcutta). 'Prosperity to it' was a toast proposed from the Chair at Blackheath and the Secretary was instructed to forward to the Captain of this new Club a copy of the Rules of the Blackheath Club. This was accordingly done through the medium of our worthy friend, Dr Charles Ferrier, under the Seal of the Club (he was appointed Doctor in the Military Service of the East India Company in November 1834). The minutes of 10 September 1826 note that Dr Ferrier brought a couple of bottles of Madeira given him at Jamaica by Mr Felling for the Club.
In October 1833 the minutes record the presence of Major Playfair as a visitor. In him Blackheath saw the founder of Golfing in the East Indies. The health of Dum Dum Golf Club (later, Calcutta), was drunk. In December 1873 the Secretary of

Royal Calcutta Clubhouse

the Calcutta Golf Club records with thanks the arrival of a handsome Gold Medal presented by the Royal Blackheath Golf Club. In December 1875 the ex-Secretary of the Calcutta Club, now living in England, records the arrival of a Silver Cup, ordered two years previously by that Club for presentation to the Royal Blackheath Golf Club. He mentions that this is the second cup made for the purpose, the first being not approved of by the Calcutta Club and therefore not sent.

Bombay Golf Club

In August 1842 the minutes state that the Blackheath Golf Club, having noticed that a Golf Club had been established in Bombay, ordered a bumper to be filled to drink success and perpetuity to the Bombay Club, and directed the Secretary to communicate this notice and to send a copy of the Rules of Blackheath Club with the intimation that their Captain was 'ex officio', an Honorary Member of the Blackheath Golf Club. The letter from the Secretary to Bombay concludes: 'Steam communication brings you at a come-atable distance, and when something more becomes to be known of the Prowess of your members, it is possible that challenges from one club to the other may be given and taken, when each will become better acquainted with the respective Links . . . the precision of steam communication warrants the indulgence of such challenges being realised.' In a reply to this letter from Bombay Golf Club, October 1842, the writer mentions that the Blackheath Medal is to be played for on St Andrews Day. He concludes his letter: 'With warmest recollections of the hospitalities which I have partaken at the Green Man Blackheath'.

In October 1843 a letter from Bombay Golf Club states that the Secretary has sent by steamer a Gold Medal resolved by the Bombay Golf Club to be presented to their Blackheath Brethren.

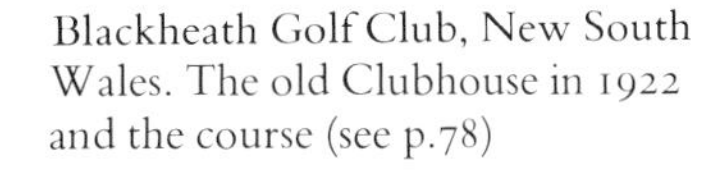

Blackheath Golf Club, New South Wales. The old Clubhouse in 1922 and the course (see p.78)

He has reason to believe that this has been lost in the wreck of the 'Memnon' and is therefore sending another, duplicate, medal.

20 February 1907. Letter from Bombay to say that their Gold Medal had been stolen. Decided to present them with a new Gold Medal.

In 1949 a letter from India states that the Bombay Golf Club had lost the land on which it had played for so many years. The Club would continue to exist and would play for its trophies on two other local courses.

It should be realised from these accounts that many members of the Bombay and Calcutta Golf Clubs were Scottish and that many clearly knew Blackheath and its members well. Finally it is interesting to point out that the Scotsmen in Bombay and Calcutta formed Golf Clubs in those places in 1830 (Calcutta) and 1842 (Bombay): whereas the first Club in England to be formed after Blackheath and Manchester (1819) appeared in 1864 at Westward Ho!.

Blackheath Golf Club, New South Wales

There is other evidence of overseas golfing connections with Captain of the New South Wales Golf Club in October 1841 on the birth of a son : the Captain, Alex Brodie Spark, is immediately the birth of a son the Captain, Alex Brodie Spark, is immediately made an Honorary Member of the Club!

The Club is situated on the highest point of the Blue Mountains of New South Wales (1035m above sea level–some 60 miles from Sydney). The Governor of New South Wales, Lachlam MacQuarie, gave Blackheath its name on 15 May 1815. His Major of Brigade, Captain H. C. Antill, described it in his diary as 'being a kind of heath but of very wild scenery'. Antill himself had been stationed at Woolwich which is adjacent to Blackheath, in England and probably suggested the name. The settlement eventually became a 'village' on 20 March 1885–just as Blackheath, in England, was similarly referred to as 'the village'.

Golf first arrived at Blackheath in 1909, petered out and appeared again with a 9-hole course in 1914. The splendid Clubhouse on the top of a hill had magnificent views over the course. The first hole descended 200 feet to the green below and the last hole was played from the depths of the valley to the heights above. A missed tee shot, however, presented an impossible task of completing the hole, together with the necessity of climbing the hill back to the Clubhouse. This enterprise was doomed to failure. The links were however saved and the present Club was started in 1922. When the foundation stone of the new Clubhouse was laid in 1924 Mr John Z. Huie stated: 'It is also historic from the fact that this Golf Club is named after the oldest Golf Club in the Empire–the Blackheath Golf Club in England where King James VI and his courtiers played golf for their recreation . . . .'

Following World War II, a close association was established between the two Clubs, food parcels were sent to the home Club and prizes were sent out. The Royal Blackheath trophies are played for annually and include two in the form of antique pewter mugs. On the same day they also play for the Hawkins and Sanderson trophies which were sent out in gratitude for the food parcels sent after the war. The Club celebrated its 60th Anniversary in 1974 in which all the trophies played for were gold. This fine 18-hole course and Clubhouse have been continually improved over the years and the Club now has no less than 820 members.

It is clear that from the best of motives Blackheath has been only too willing to help any group of golfers who wished to form or who had just formed, a Golf Club. In England they seem to have had particular interest in the start of Westward Ho! (1864), Hoylake (1867), the Wimbledon course (1865)–later to be Royal Wimbledon and Wimbledon Common–and, at a later date, Great Yarmouth.

There is much evidence to show how keen Blackheath were in their support of these Clubs.

Royal North Devon Golf Club

Royal North Devon (Westward Ho!) founded in 1864, was the first to appear and therefore got most attention. Although the journey from Blackheath to North Devon was long, Blackheath golfers lost no time in appearing on the North Devon scene, playing in matches and competitions, presenting fine prizes and joining Westward Ho! as members. On the Honours' Boards at Westward Ho! George Glennie won the Club Gold Medal in 1865 (the first Year), 1866 and 1867, H. A. Lamb in 1872 and Col. E. H. Kennard won it in 1873. The Prince of Wales Medal, later the King Edward VII Medal, was won by Sir Robert Hay Bart. in

Group at Westward Ho! *c.* 1870, showing the Iron Hut, which was then the Clubhouse

Royal North Devon (Westward Ho!) Clubhouse today

1868 (the inaugural year), 1869 and 1874.

The Trophies–Lieut. General Moncrieff's Challenge Silver Cross was presented by him in 1864, the Lindsay-Bennet Gold Medals were presented, for the Ladies 1868 and for the Men 1881, and the Blackheath Badge was presented in 1871.

Not only were Blackheath members winners and presenters of prizes but some became important members of Westward Ho!.

In 1873 Lieut.-Col. Kennard was President; in 1874 Sir Robert Hay and in 1875 James Lindsay-Bennet.

Hoylake (Royal Liverpool Golf Club)

The inaugural meeting, forming the Club, was held in May 1869. The first golf meeting was held in October 1869. At this meeting J. W. Adamson (Captain Blackheath 1867) and Mr Walker played and, on the second day, represented Blackheath in an inter-Club foursome Competition.

The second Captain of Hoylake was Col. E. H. Kennard; he was in office for two years and, during this time, he persuaded H.R.H. the Duke of Connaught to become President of the Club and this led to the Club being allowed to adopt the prefix 'Royal'. Kennard gave the 'Kennard Gold Medal' for the best scratch score of the second day of the Autumn Meeting, in 1871.

Both George Glennie and G. D. Brown won scratch medals at Hoylake but the most successful Blackheath golfer was H. M. P. Buskin, a winner of the Spring Medal at Blackheath on six occasions and of the Summer Medal on four occasions, who won no less than five scratch Medals at Hoylake, between 1871 and 1873.

The Great Yarmouth Club

The Great Yarmouth Club was founded in 1882 by Dr Thomas Browne. He got off to an unpromising start, as a meeting called by him to discuss the project was attended only by himself. He therefore elected himself Captain, Treasurer and Secretary and immediately afterwards accepted two challenges to a team match. The greatest factor in the subsequent success of the Club was the support at once accorded to it by Royal Blackheath Golf Club members. The 'Penn' Medal (John Penn of Blackheath) was played for in 1887 and the Blackheath Medal was presented by

Above:
Royal Hotel, Hoylake. Part of this hotel was the first Clubhouse of the Royal Liverpool Golf Club when it was formed

Royal Liverpool Clubhouse (Hoylake) today

Royal Blackheath in 1893. Many Blackheath members joined the Club and five of them became Captains of Great Yarmouth. Great Yarmouth records: 'Under their [Blackheath] guidance, the ceremonial at Yarmouth Club developed. At every annual dinner the Yarmouth players could be seen in their picturesque red coats, similar to those worn at Blackheath . . . The ceremony of the swearing-in of the Captain has been handed down in a similar way'. Robert Whyte (1848–1931) was a founder member and was Captain of Great Yarmouth in 1892–93; he was also a Captain of Blackheath and was Field Marshal of Blackheath 1913–1930.

In 1898 members of Great Yarmouth, who were not members of Royal Blackheath also, sent a gift of £25 to Blackheath suggesting that the Club buy a prize. They said that they felt this was a graceful and fitting act for all the help that the Great Yarmouth Golf Club had received in the past from Royal Blackheath Golf Club. The money was used by Blackheath to buy a silver rose-water dish, which was named The Great Yarmouth Bowl and is played for annually.

The close connection of Royal Blackheath with these two Clubs is repeated both at Wimbledon and Hoylake.

Royal Wimbledon Golf Club

At Wimbledon, an early feature after the founding of what was, at that time, the London Scottish Club, was the annual match against Blackheath.

Among members common to both Clubs were Dr W. Laidlaw Purves and Mr H. A. Lamb. The latter was Secretary to the Wimbledon Club for 14 years and, as Secretary, saw them through the difficult and acrimonious times which ended in the Wimbledon Golf Club and the London Scottish Golf Club becoming separate entities. In this troubled time, he was supported by the then Captain, George Moncrieff.

Royal St George's Golf Club

Royal St George's (Sandwich), like Wimbledon, had considerable support in its very earliest days from H. A. Lamb and Dr W. Laidlaw Purves and there is a Lamb Memorial Medal for the absolute best scratch score of the year at either the Spring or Autumn Meetings; in respect of these two gentlemen, perhaps primarily members of Royal Wimbledon, though also members of Blackheath, it could be said that Royal Wimbledon was much concerned with the start of Royal St George's and Laidlaw Purves was the first Captain from 1887–89; but Cornelius Thomson and Col. Kennard were also founder members and Robert Whyte was an original ordinary member: Kennard was later Captain of Royal St George's, also. It is thus clear that, as usual, Blackheath was vigorous and active in nurturing yet another offspring.

At Rye, F. S. Ireland was an original member; at Minchinhampton, in Gloucestershire, Mr Ritchie of Blackheath was a founder member. Blackheath played a part in founding Royal Epping Golf Club, Littlestone Golf Club, Dartford Heath Golf Club and Barnehurst Golf Club. Probably Blackheath was associated, through its members, with the founding of many other English Clubs, of which we have no record, but enough has been said to show that Blackheath was an originator, and keen, active supporter of nearly all the earlier English Clubs and was effectively the father of English golf and of golf in the Far East.

Chapter 6 Blackheath in the late nineteenth and early twentieth centuries

By 1875 Blackheath was a prosperous and famous Golf Club and had a justifiable claim to have some famous and respected golfers. Their excellent organisation had steadily improved the golf course and Clubhouse. At this time the membership included not only golfers and important local men but also Peers of the Realm, Members of Parliament and important merchants of the City. Such men as:

Viscount Dupplin
The Earl of Eglinton
The Duke of Beaufort
Viscount Dalrymple
Sir Hugh Hume-Campbell–Captain 1850
Rt. Hon. Sir Stuart Knill
Sir Thomas Moncrieffe
Sir Francis Grant PRA (who painted Field Marshal Lindsay's Portrait)
Edward Hughes (elected 1854–author of *Chronicles of Blackheath Golfers*, Captain 1893–94; Secretary & Treasurer 1891/3)

The Rt. Hon. Sir Stuart Knill became Lord Mayor of London in 1893 and entertained Blackheath Golf Club to dinner at the Mansion House, the first (and probably the last) time that a Golf Club has been so honoured. This dinner was a worthy successor to the great dinners of the old days being of 7 courses, no doubt accompanied by suitable wines and–added grandeur–a Police Band played during dinner followed, after dinner, by a recital of songs with piano accompanist, the last song (of eight) seems, after such a dinner, very appropriate – 'Soft may thy slumbers be.' The Club, as a token of gratitude, allowed Mr Richard Winch to present the Knill Cup to commemorate the event. The Club had Edward, Prince of Wales, as Patron of the Club in 1899 and presented H.R.H. with a copy of the *Chronicles of Blackheath Golfers*. When Edward became King Edward VII in 1901 the Club sought and got the King's patronage and in the same year the King graciously acceded to the request of the Club to be allowed to use the prefix 'Royal'.

Although it may well seem that the Club had now become the greatest in England, prosperous, mellow, full of tradition and destined for greater glories, it was beset with troubles and

A panoramic view of Eltham Golf Club and its members *c.* 1894 (see p. 93)

difficulties which had slowly accumulated over 30 years. These stemmed from the growth of London, the urbanisation of Blackheath and the increase in road traffic. In addition, the position of Blackheath as the first of few golf courses in England had changed; the golf explosion had arrived.

In 1850 there were 17 Golf Clubs and Societies in the United Kingdom (of which only two were in England). In 1870 there were 34; in 1890, 387 and in 1910, 4,135. The great majority were of 18 holes; styles of golf architecture had changed. At that time Blackheath still had 7 holes; the long policy of filling in the gravel pits, cutting the whins and improving both tees and green had resulted in a pleasant, old-fashioned and less formidable golf course. The Heath was busier, traffic much heavier and use by the general public was much greater. These problems had grown slowly and inexorably for a long time. In June 1856 the minutes record an accident to a passer-by, hit by a golf ball. It was at this time that forecaddies became obligatory. In August 1871 the Metropolitan Board of Works, through its representative Mr Smith, proposed a bye-law 'that the golfers should steer clear of the cricketer's green'. Resolved that, in the summer, the course should be changed so as not to interfere with established cricket clubs.

In October 1879 a Mr Richardson of the Metropolitan Board of Works stated that a friend of his had been struck by a golf ball while walking on one of the beaten paths on the Heath. In May 1890 the LCC wrote to report on an accident and requested the Club to discontinue the long hole which was played on Medal Days. The Club acceded.

In October 1892 three members wrote to the Committee expressing concern over the crowded state of the Heath and desiring an extraordinary general meeting to consider the future of the course. Nothing came of this. In 1894 a golf magazine reported that Blackheath had a number of 'daily breaders' i.e. those who played golf before breakfast, and stated that as many as 20 couples drove off, starting at 7 a.m. in the summer or as soon as it was light in the winter. The same magazine also pointed out that, at Bank Holiday time, the public picniced in large numbers on the Heath, frequently chosing the putting greens to play 'Kiss in the Ring'.

In 1894 golf was only played on Blackheath on Tuesdays, Thursdays and Saturdays up to 2 p.m. On all other days play was difficult after lunch and a forecaddie essential. New local rules had to be made to allow balls to be lifted off roads, away from sewer ventilators, fixed seats, lamp posts, etc. At the turn of the century it was contemptuously observed that the 'principal hazards on the Hazard Course are lamp posts and nursemaids'. In 1901 F. S. Ireland suggested an alternative course but nothing came of it. Despite the various problems concerned with overcrowding and the encroachment by the general public, the course was still a difficult one. In 1910 Bernard Darwin said that the lies were hard and flinty and the course was a tough one, particularly because the two very long and difficult holes were consecutive. He mentioned that he had to play in a red coat, had to have a forecaddie and that there was constant danger of slaughtering pedestrians and old gentlemen sitting on public seats. He concluded that the course was a good test of golf and that three rounds on Blackheath on a cold, blustery day was man's work.

The Blackheath Tercentenary

This was celebrated by a Dinner at the Cecil Hotel on 2 April 1908 (Spring Medal Day). It was a great event–detailed Club records of it seem not to have survived but it was reported in the newspapers. There were many guests, including the Captains of: the Royal and Ancient, Hoylake, Royal North Devon (Westward Ho!), Royal Wimbledon, Great Yarmouth, Royal Bombay, Royal Calcutta and Royal St George's Golf Clubs. Also there were Horace Hutchinson, H. S. C. Everard of St Andrews, eminent golfer and golf historian, Dunbar Duncan Chairman of the LCC, Alfred Lyttelton MP, A. S. Balfour, MP, the Editor of the *Times*, and the Editor of the *Kentish Mercury*. At this time the membership of Royal Blackheath was 105 but the total number at the Dinner was 240, so it was a prodigious turn-out of members and guests. The Field Marshal, Col. E. H. Kennard, was present

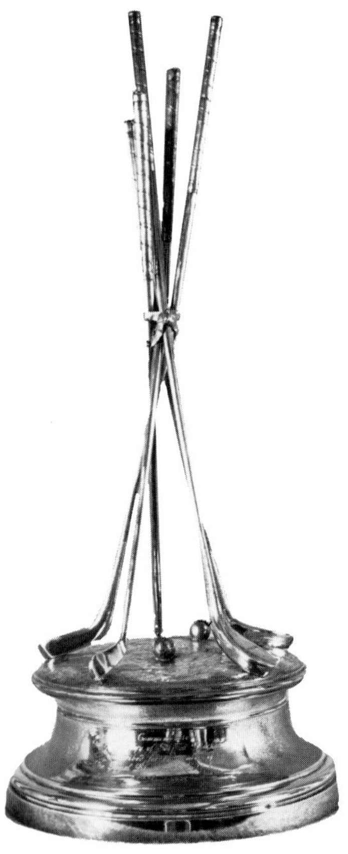

The Tercentenary Silver Memento

(by then he had been a member for over 50 years) as were (no doubt among many other past-Captains) R. Winch, Captain 1908, J. S. Sawyer, Captain 1907 and A. C. Latter, Captain Elect for 1909. The tables were arranged to denote that the Club had attained its 300th anniversary. The head table marked 'Third' and the others with seven letters to make up the word 'Century'.

As part of the celebration a print of a portrait of James I was bought and a Tercentenary Medal was devised. This consisted of a gold coin of James I's reign encircled by a gold band. The band was inscribed on one side 'Royal Blackheath Golf Club 1908' and on the other 'Tercentenary Medal 1608'. This was the Captain's Badge and was to be worn by him at Wee Dinners and other official occasions. The Club sent loyal greetings to their Patron, His Majesty the King. They had a Tercentenary piece of silver made. This consisted of four golf clubs, standing on a plinth of silver. The clubs were held at the centre by a strap and splayed out above and below. There was a cleek, with no name and three wooden clubs, each marked, Dunn, Hunter and Kirk. There were three golf balls on the plinth, respectively a feathery, a gutta and a bramble-marked rubber core. The total height of the trophy is at least 2 feet.

Because of the occasion and the presence of the press, the newspapers made much of it. Henry Leach wrote an article in *Fry's Magazine*, giving a summary of the historical background and extolling the virtues of Royal Blackheath and the course. The *Graphic* devoted three pages to it. The Club has nothing in the minutes but there is a photo of the Dinner: the only other existing memento is a menu card in one of the scrap books. There is no record of the speeches.

In July 1908, Braid, Taylor and Harry Vardon, with brother Tom Vardon, played a stroke competition over the 21-hole round. Taylor won with 96 strokes, which seems to confirm the difficulty and toughness of the course, as described by Bernard Darwin. In the afternoon, in a better ball four-ball match in which Braid and Taylor played the Vardons, the latter won. Although the minute books do not specifically state it, there can be little doubt that this exhibition match was also part of the Tercentenary celebration.

On 6 July 1909 The Royal Blackheath moved into their new Clubhouse–Heath (or Heath Hill) House.

On 15 September 1914, it was resolved to postpone all competitions and Wee Dinners until further notice. 15 guineas was voted to the Prince of Wales National Relief Fund. It was also resolved to make the Territorial Officer guarding the Blackheath Railway Station an Honorary Member.

On 23 February 1915, the Hon. Secretary reported that the members of the Royal Blackheath Golf Club had been made Honorary Members of the Eltham Golf Club until the termination of the War. The First World War gave the final *coup de grâce* to the course, although matches were still played on it after World War I and even the occasional medal. An extraordinary general meeting was held on 13 October 1921 to consider the future of the Royal Blackheath Golf Club.

A Foursome in 1908 (the year of the Tercentenary). Colonel Kennard on the left, next to him W. E. Hughes, author of the *Chronicles*.

Some Blackheath notables (1844–1908)

It may seem invidious to select a few men from among the many distinguished and active golfers and administrators of golf who existed in the heyday of Blackheath, but the authors feel that there were four men in this part of the Club's history who made outstanding contributions to the welfare and development of Blackheath and of golf in England generally.

Lieut. Col. Edmund Hegan Kennard (1836–1912)

He was elected a member of Blackheath Golf Club in 1852. Kennard was from Hackney not far distant from Blackheath being educated at Dr Powles's School on the Heath overlooking the course. The Rev. William Marsh, Chaplain of Morden College, a keen member of Blackheath and winner of the Summer and Spring Medals of 1849, 50 and 51, took an interest in him (and in Jelf Sharp also at the School) and would arrange games with the two boys, himself and Willie Dunn from time to time. As a result, Kennard developed a good swing which stood him in good stead all his life. He won the Boys' Medal in 1850. After joining the Club he won the Spring Medal in 1864; subsequently he won five more, the last being in 1883, thirty years after winning the first. At one time and another he won all the Scratch Medals of the Club. He went to Balliol College, Oxford, and, in sport, he distinguished himself at Racquets,

Portrait of Colonel Kennard (taken from the picture 'Golf at Blackheath' 1875)

Portrait of Colonel Kennard (from the Frontispiece of *Chronicles of Blackheath Golfers*)

winning both the gold and silver racquets. In 1858 he graduated and then joined the Queen's Own 7th Regiment of Light Dragoons, so that for some years he was busy with his Army career and served abroad. In 1874/5 he was MP for Lymington. He became a member of Westward Ho! in 1870 and there won Lieut.-General Moncrieff's Silver Challenge Cross in 1870 and the Club Gold Medal in 1873. He was elected President of Royal North Devon (Westward Ho!) in 1873. In 1870, be became a founder member of Hoylake and was Captain of that Club in 1872 and 73.

In 1873 he joined the Wimbledon Golf Club: he presented them with a Gold Medal to play for and was Captain of that Club in 1882. In 1868 he joined St Andrews and was a regular player in the Autumn Meeting although he never won a medal. On one occasion he was ten shots in the lead with two holes to play, but took nine at the Road Hole having had trouble in the Stationmaster's garden. He was a founder member of Royal St George's and subsequently its Captain. He was Captain of Blackheath in 1875 and was elected Field Marshal in 1894. He was one of the original 500 subscribers to the first edition of Robert Clark's *Golf, a Royal and Ancient Game*. In November 1903 he had been a member of Blackheath for 50 years and a Dinner was held in his honour at the Ship Hotel in Greenwich. To celebrate his fifty years he presented the Club with a silver cup: the Jubilee Cup. He was a man renowned for playing the game for the game's sake; the best of golfing partners and the most courteous opponent; always proud to be a winner nevertheless he did not

George Glennie putting (from an oil painting by Heywood Hardy RA in Blackheath Clubhouse)

consider this important and was wont to deplore, in later life, the loss of due reverence for the game that he had known in his youth. He must have been a great figure at the Tercentenary Dinner: as Field Marshal, with 55 years as a Blackheath member. He died in November 1912.

George Glennie
(1818–1886)

A civil engineer and an ironmaster from Glasgow and who was, at one time, manager of the Monkland Canal Co., Montrose, Scotland, was elected a member in 1853 and immediately made his mark as a golfer. In 1854 he won his first Spring Medal and won again in 1855, 63 and 65. He won the Summer Medal six times–1859, 60, 61, 63, 64, 65 and the Bombay Medal 1858, 59, 64 and 67. Like many of his contemporaries, he did not confine his golf to Blackheath, winning the Club Gold Medal at Westward Ho! in 1865, 66, 67 and the King William IV Gold Medal of the R. & A. in 1855 with a score of 88, which score was unbeaten for 35 years. In 1851 he won the Silver Medal of the Royal and Ancient. It is clear that he was an accomplished golfer before he came to Blackheath and had learnt his game in Scotland.

Undoubtedly, as far as Blackheath are concerned, the highlight of his career was his winning of the Grand Tournament at St Andrews in 1857. This was a foursome Tournament and he played with Captain Stewart of the 72nd Highlanders. They won decisively, beating the R. & A. in the Final convincingly and Blackheath made them both Life Members on the strength of it. In order to appreciate the wonder of their victory, the reader must remember that golf came from Scotland and that, at this time, Blackheath was the only Golf Club in England, apart from Manchester, and Blackheath was the only competitor from outside Scotland. Perhaps it was some sop to Scottish pride that both were Scots and had learnt their golf in Scotland. Capt. Stewart had won the King William IV Gold Medal of the R. & A. in 1853, two years before Glennie did. Glennie was the local hero and Stewart, also, though the latter never seems to have courted fame and his part tends to be forgotten.

In 1862 and 63 Glennie was Captain of Blackheath and when Captain Crosse, the Secretary of the Club, died in 1868, Glennie was unanimously elected Secretary and Treasurer and continued so until his death in 1886. He transferred his energies to the Club Secretaryship and was indefatigable in his efforts. Among many achievements, he and James Lindsay-Bennett were responsible, both financially and administratively, for setting up a billiard room and acquiring a billiard table. Glennie advanced £100 of his own money into this and subsequently wrote to the Club to say that he hoped to get the money back, but that, if he should die before this happened, his heirs and successors would not claim it and the Club might have the sum as a gift. It was during the period 1868–86 that such strenuous efforts were made to improve the course and in which Clubhouse facilities were generally improved. There can be little doubt that Glennie was a good administrator and a man of some force of character. In 1875 the Club had instituted prizes for score play under handicap. There was no record of a 'bogey' (old time equivalent of a standard scratch score) and it is said that, when Secretary, Glennie sat in the Clubhouse during the play of the Medal and, having regard to the weather and the condition of the course, worked out each player's handicap for that day. So no competitor knew what his handicap was until he got back to the Clubhouse! In October 1881 the Club honoured Glennie for his services as Secretary by having the George Glennie Medal struck. Two medals were made, one was sent to the R. & A. for annual competition and one was kept by Blackheath for annual competition. On 27 October 1881 at a Dinner at the Ship Hotel at Greenwich a golfing picture by Mr Heywood Hardy RA of a group of golfers, with Glennie predominating, but John Penn, Francis Gilbert, William McCandlish and 'Dick' Steer, an old caddie, also included, was presented to the Club by Mr John Aird, in honour of Glennie. Glennie died, in harness, on 27 March 1886, and in April of that year the Club subscribed to a memorial stone to be placed over his grave. A portrait of Glennie, seated and holding a cleek, was painted by John Ballentyne RSA and was presented to the Club by Mr Archibald Hamilton: it hangs in the Clubhouse today.

Frederick Schomberg Ireland (1861–1937)

Ireland became a Blackheath member in about 1887. He had a brother, George, who was also a member of Blackheath. Like

F. S. Ireland

Kennard, Ireland was a local man and learnt to play at Blackheath but, unlike Kennard, he does not seem to have started golf at an early age. He was a man of many parts and a good athlete. He played cricket before he took up golf and played for Kent on several occasions; he was Hon. Sec. of the Blackheath Cricket Club 1885–91. He played rugby to a good Club standard and played full back for Blackheath 1878/79. He was known locally as a skilled fisherman and a good shot.

He had other talents than the athletic, being an above average violinist and also composed music–one waltz, in particular, that he composed became very popular.

He turned to golf and had some tuition in 1887 from Anderson, then professional at Blackheath. In 1888 he was runner-up in the Singapore Cup; in 1891 he tied for the Spring Medal and in 1892 won the Photographic Society Medal and the Bombay Medal. In 1893 he was runner-up in the Spring Medal and in that year he went abroad. On his return, he immediately took up where he had left off. He won the Spring Medal in 1895, 96, 97; the Summer Medal in 1895, 96 and his winning score in 1895 of 101 was a record for the course. He won the Bombay

Medal in 1896, 97; the Photographic Society's Medal, 1891, 94, 95, 96 and the George Glennie Medal 1895, 96. In 1896 his handicap was +5, but he still won the Penn Cup off this handicap. He played in the Amateur Championship at Royal St George's and got through two rounds 'though unwell'. In November 1896 Blackheath played Cambridge University and Ireland defeated Bernard Darwin (an undergraduate) by 5 holes. He was a founder member of Rye Golf Club and in 1898 was Captain of Great Yarmouth.

In 1895 and 96 he was Captain of Royal Blackheath and suggested, in 1895, that the ladies of the Blackheath Ladies' Club be invited to view the plate, pictures, etc.; light refreshments to be provided. Consideration of this was deferred by the Committee.

He was elected Secretary of Royal Blackheath in April 1898 and resigned that office in July 1902. He was asked to continue to serve on the Committee. In 1902 he moved to Mildenhall, Essex. Ultimately he went to live in Menton, S. France and died there, completely forgotten, in 1937.

W. E. Hughes, author of *Chronicles of Blackheath Golfers*. Hon. Sec. 1891–2; Captain 1893

W. E. Hughes

Last, but by no means least, W. E. Hughes should be remembered as a notable member of Blackheath. He was elected Honorary Secretary and Treasurer on 14 April 1891 and remained in office until 1893. In 1893 he was Captain of Blackheath. He won the Penn Cup in 1891 and 94, playing off a handicap of 6 in 1891 and 8 in 1894; so he was a capable, if not expert golfer. He produced his *Chronicles of Blackheath Golfers* in 1897 at his own expense and, in the preface, hopes 'that this volume may commend itself not only to fellow Blackheath Golfers but also to brother Golfers at large, as a slight contribution to the history of the ancient game'. The book is dedicated to Col. Kennard and to the Committee.

Chapter 7 Blackheath after World War I The amalgamation

If it was clear before World War I that Blackheath could not continue to play on its own Heath, it was even more clear after the war and between 1920 and 1923 Blackheath made attempts to merge with its neighbour, Eltham Golf Club, about three miles away. Eltham Golf Club had always been a good neighbour and had allowed Blackheath the use of its course during World War I.

Although they had to give up their golf course they did not contemplate giving up their Clubhouse–Heath House–which remained in their possession for another 26 years.

History of Eltham Golf Club

The Club came into existence in March 1892 and had a golf course in a pleasant park surrounding Eltham Lodge. This Lodge was the Clubhouse and both course and Clubhouse were (and still are) leased from the Crown. If the Eltham course was pleasant but not distinguished, the Clubhouse was magnificent. A Royal castle or manor had existed in the area from the fourteenth century. In 1356 the Black Prince sent his father to the Palace at Eltham. In 1387 King Richard II retired to Eltham Palace. Elizabeth Tudor, 2nd daughter of Henry VIII, was born there on 2 July 1492 and died there on 14 November 1495. Subsequently Elizabeth I resided there, but infrequently as she had a palace at nearby Greenwich. The present building, Eltham Lodge, was built in 1664 on the site of one of the lodges in the great park that surrounded the moated palace. The building was commissioned by Sir John Shaw and the architect was Hugh May: the latter was a considerable financier and an architect of outstanding ability. He was a contemporary of Sir Christopher Wren, but he studied architecture in Holland while in exile with the Duke of Buckingham and this probably accounts for the Dutch influence in his design. The front of Eltham Lodge is a facsimile of the famous Mauritshuis at The Hague. A feature of his domestic style of architecture is a general absence of corridors, well exemplified in Eltham Lodge. The building is a good example of mid seventeenth-century Renaissance architecture but a lot of alteration took place in the first half of the eighteenth century. As an example, the original windows were stone-mullioned but only three windows of this style remain, at basement level. The Shaw family continued to live in Eltham Lodge until 1830, when the property reverted to the Crown. The Crown then leased the property to a Mr Wood, a hop merchant. He arranged for his wife to continue with the lease, if she survived him. She did this and lived to be 99. In 1891 Eltham Golf Club took over the lease of both Lodge and Park. Some very old tapestries, discovered underneath old wallpaper,

The front of Blackheath Clubhouse

were subsequently removed to the British Museum. The Clubhouse contains many oil portraits of the Shaw family. The Eltham Golf Club had adopted as its Club badge a rampant horse and the legend 'Invicta', this being the old emblem of the men of Kent: this badge and legend they inscribed on their medals.

This, then, was the Club which was considering a merger with the Royal Blackheath Golf Club in 1920–23. As might be imagined there were some doubts on both sides and, on the Eltham side, the early demand by Royal Blackheath that the amalgamated Club should keep their title, must have caused some misgivings. There were problems, too, about responsibility for the two Clubhouses (Royal Blackheath were keeping Heath House on), about who should be allowed to play in the competitions of either Club, about the position of debenture holders and about the amount of subscription (Eltham's was higher than Royal Blackheath's). There was friction but, eventually, in 1923 agreement was reached and a new lease was negotiated in that year between the Crown and the Royal Blackheath Golf Club for Eltham Lodge and the course. That agreement was reached was in no small measure due to Christian Gray of Royal Blackheath and John Eagleton of Eltham Golf

Heath House

Club: both were on the negotiating committee and both were firm friends who liked and trusted one another.

When the merger took place C. H. Gray was elected Captain and John Eagleton was elected to the Committee. Colonel Rich was to be the Hon. Secretary. In the year following John Eagleton was elected Captain. The position at the time of the merger was that the course was run jointly, as the Royal Blackheath Golf Club, with the Blackheath badge and legend. Each Clubhouse was run by a Sub-committee, elected from the original members of each Club, but, whereas the Eltham Clubhouse continued as a Golf Clubhouse for Blackheath and Eltham, the Royal Blackheath Clubhouse became a social club where billiards and bridge were played and it was looked after by Mr & Mrs Moore, who lived in Heath House Cottage, adjoining. Mr Moore had been Field Marshal Robert Whyte's butler and had expressed a wish that he and his wife should be Steward and Stewardess, to which Robert Whyte agreed. They remained there until they were retired, on grounds of old age, in 1929.

Christian Gray, as Captain, supported by John Eagleton, set about cementing the union of the two Clubs under one name and the years 1923 and 1924 were eventful. In 1923 a letter to the LCC stated that the Club no longer intended to maintain the greens on the old course. In 1923 the Committee decided not to let the Eltham course for the grazing of sheep. Guy Eagleton tells an interesting tale about the grazing rights. The idea stemmed from Scotland and a Scots farmer paid £60 a year for the right to graze. The farmer sent his flock down in the charge of a shepherd, for whom the Club provided a hut, which stood on the south side of the wood by the 18th green and from here the shepherd had a wide view of the course. Eagleton recalls that the sheep grazed both fairways and greens, to the detriment of the latter, and that both sheep and lambs did much damage to the bunkers, which the former used as a dry place to lie and the latter as a playground. After a few months at Eltham, the sheep were taken to graze in one of the London parks and from there were sold for slaughter.

1923
The Royal Artillery Mess, Woolwich, asked permission to use the ground at Barnehurst 'formerly used as the ladies golf links' as a polo ground.

1923
The ladies (who were allowed to play on the course 'if they had suitable handicaps') were allowed to use the main dining-room for meals 'subject to such conditions as to time of use as the Committee may decide'.

1923
Agreed to purchase a motor tractor mower to supersede the horsedrawn one. This was a good move, as, in 1924, the Hon. Secretary reported that the horse had been 'called up for military duty'.

1924
Crown Lease was renewed.

1924
Mr Christian Gray offered £2,000 towards course alterations but stipulated that the alterations be done as recommended by James Braid or such other course architect that he approved of.

1924
Mr C. Gray gave two silver cups to the Royal Blackheath Golf Club for presentation to the Chantilly G.C. and the La Baule G.C., in France.

1924
Mrs Gray presented a bracelet to the Royal Blackheath Golf Club for presentation to the Kent County Ladies' Golf Association to be called the Royal Blackheath Bracelet.

1924
A Mr Goodwin of Budleigh Salterton offered to sell the Club a coloured engraving of The Golfers of Blackheath. 'As these engravings are of no value', the Club declined.

1924
Royal Blackheath heartily approved the suggested formation of a Kent County Golf Union.

1925
Royal Blackheath joined the Kent County Golf Union. It is noted that an increasing number of Golf Societies were beginning to use the Club for meetings.

1925
Royal Blackheath presented a silver cup to the Kent County Golf Union which was to be for the individual amateur championship.

Between 1925 and 1929 quite extensive alterations were carried out on the course, mainly on suggestions made by James Braid.

1926
(April) The Committee agreed that all American visitors visiting the Club, under the auspices of the Cunard Line, would be given vouchers issued by the Line and that all debts will be settled by Cunard.

1928
C. H. Gray presented the Honours Board for the Medals and the list of Field Marshals, which make a handsome adornment to the 19th-hole bar.

1930
C. H. Gray was invested as Field Marshal (Robert Whyte asked to be retired owing to age and infirmity. He had been Field Marshal from 1913–1930.)

1932
C. H. Gray presented the Gray Putting Cup.

1933
The Artisans' Club was formed.

In pursuing its custom of encouraging golf and golf competition, the Royal Blackheath Golf Club gave a Silver Cup, together with an illuminated address, to the Fédération Française de Golf, to be the Challenge Cup in a National Amateur Foursome competition. This Cup was gratefully accepted and has been played for annually ever since, with a gap during World War II. The original trophy disappeared during the German Occupation, but, after the war, the Fédération Française produced another Cup and the competition continues as one of the leading Open Amateur events in the French calendar.

Royal Blackheath also established a link with the Kenya Golfing Society shortly after its formation in 1930. This association owed much to H. F. Eagleton, (younger son of John Eagleton) who won the Kenya Championship in 1930. The Club donated to the Kenya Golfing Society a silver cup to be called the Royal Blackheath Trophy, to be played for annually for foursome play under handicap. From 1931 until World War II members of the Kenya Golfing Society on leave in the UK played a regular annual match against Royal Blackheath.

In 1934 a photograph of the Blackheath Golf Club in the Blue Mountain's, near Sydney, New South Wales, Australia, was gratefully received from Mr John E. Hine, Hon. Secretary of that Club. The letter from the Blackheath Golf Club, which is 80 miles from Sydney, Australia, states the Royal Blackheath Golf Club has long associations with its Australian counterpart and that at some time R.B.G.C. had presented them with 12 silver ashtrays and a copy of Hughes' *Chronicles*. They state that the copy of the *Chronicles* is carefully preserved and opened each day at a fresh page (see Chapter 5, p.78).

Blackheath continued on an even and uneventful path through the 1930s. In 1937 the Territorial Army requested a site for an Anti-Aircraft Searchlight Company and one by the Green Lane entrance to the Club was agreed. In 1939 came World War II.

Some notes on the Royal Blackheath course at Eltham

The course is a pleasant parkland course which has been shrewdly landscaped and planted with trees: the variety and beauty of the trees (some of which are very old) is a feature of a course of good turf and greens, which is a trifle flat and rather on the short side. The course boasts three decorative water hazards, in the form of ponds. In recent years, alas, it has lost all of its large and beautiful elm trees but replacement of these by other trees is well under way and although the course has a railway along one boundary and many houses and a block of flats near it, these are all well concealed and, when playing, one could well think oneself in the countryside. The course is well bunkered and by no means easy but its greatest virtue is that it has that most desirable quality of any course–it is a delightful course on which to play. The last two holes have considerable character; the 17th with a cross bunker, a

Eighteenth green and defending hedge, with a view of the back of the Clubhouse

remnant of the great days of the gutty, which although resulting in a half-blind second, gives the player a satisfying carry, is followed by the 18th–267 yards to a green defended by a ditch and a hedge of considerable thickness; except for a small gap at the left corner which is guarded by a sand bunker. To complete these holes and then to enter the magnificent and friendly Clubhouse is a most fitting end to a pleasant round of golf.

Christian Gray (Died, 1932)

Christian Gray lived in the Blackheath area and was Chairman of the India Rubber Gutta Percha Co. which had its factory–called Silvertown–in North Woolwich. This factory was a leading factory in the early days of motor tyres; the company produced the Palmer Cord Tyre and was an original producer of gutty balls, i.e. composite gutta balls, of which the best known was the hard, resilient, Silvertown No. 4, a good golf ball in its time but which caused much damage, by its hardness, to the old wooden golf clubfaces (see p. 121). The business was a family business and there was another factory near Paris.

Christian Gray was a wealthy man and a great benefactor to Royal Blackheath because he believed passionately in the prestige of Royal Blackheath and its importance as a leader in the golf world. He was elected a member in 1903. In 1908 he is said to have played an important part in organising the exhibition match played by Braid, Taylor and the two Vardons, which was part of the Tercentenary Celebrations. Golf was not his only interest and as a young man he played Rugger for Blackheath; he told his friends that in his day it was a pretty rough, damaging, game, played in jersey, knickerbockers and thick stockings which protected the shins. He did not confine his golfing activities to

Christian Gray

Blackheath, being very partial to France and to golfing there: he had, at one time, a holiday house at Rye and frequently played there. He was the first Captain of Royal Blackheath after the amalgamation, in 1923, and was elected Field Marshal in 1930.

As has been mentioned in the Club history, he gave generously and did much to promote the Royal Blackheath name in France. He not only paid for the Trophy given to the Fédération Française de Golf for an international foursome competition, but took a team of six, entirely at his own expense, to play in the first staging of that event. He had a brother, Bill (W. E. Gray) who was also a keen and prominent Blackheath member and who served on the Committee. It was due to Christian Gray's personality and to the personality of his great friend John Eagleton, an Eltham member originally, that the amalgamation of Royal Blackheath and Eltham finally took place despite general opposition and misgivings on the part of many members of both Clubs.

John Eagleton's son, Guy Eagleton, has personal recollections of him in the 1920s when, he says, 'I used to pay a visit to the Club on my return from the City and would find the brothers sitting in their corner, where now stands the one-armed bandit, absorbing Scotch in quiet contemplation. They had come by train to Eltham station where Chris's Rolls-Royce awaited them.'

His portrait hangs in the dining-room, painted by Cohen, a fitting tribute to one who gave of his time and money to the Club, of which he was justly proud to be a member.

William Fanstone Dyer
(1899–1964)

Born 1899. He was a local man and, as a boy, played on the Heath before World War I. After completing his education, he joined his father's firm of local Estate Agents, in Montpelier Road, Blackheath. He was a great supporter of Blackheath, giving to it both his time and money. Using his expertise as an Estate Agent, he conducted negotiations with the Crown Agents, on behalf of the Club, concerning the lease liability for repairs to the Clubhouse, in particular, after bomb damage in World War II. The actual damage caused by the bomb was slight, though it destroyed the putting green, but when the house was inspected, the floor of the billiard room was found to be weakened, the south wall required attention and there was a large amount of rotting timber to be replaced. He persuaded the Crown Agents not only to undertake the necessary repairs but also, at the same time, to replace some of the interior of the house to make it more suitable for use as a Clubhouse. The re-planning was the work of Jock Stevenson and he was aided and supported throughout by Dyer.

Although Dyer could not play much golf, he played a lot of snooker, at which he was very expert. He was a class player and frequent winner of the tournament. His two sisters helped and encouraged him in his support of the Club and he arranged for them to live in the house behind the old Clubhouse (Heath House). When the last surviving sister died, the house was sold and the proceeds given to the Club.

In another walk of life he became Master of the Worshipful Company of Haberdashers. His generosity to the Club was considerable and he bought the dining-room carpet: in his will he left a legacy to what he called the Captain's Fund. The conditions were that the Trustees were to ensure that all the investments were in their name and that all income was to be spent on projects to maintain the furnishings. They were also given a wider discretion in giving support to Club projects which were beyond what the Club was in a position to undertake. The amount of this legacy is not disclosed but it is regarded as his most generous gift, by far. He was Captain of the Club 1939–45 and did much to keep things going during the war years and, as has been said, to get the Clubhouse maintained and repaired after the war. During World War II he not only continued the annual Captain's Dinner but paid for it, as well. (See illustration on p.22.)

He became Field Marshal in 1959 and remained so until his death in 1964. While he was Field Marshal the Captains suggested that they would pay for his portrait to be painted, but he would have none of it and insisted instead upon a picture of the Field Marshal, the Captain and all the past-Captains at a Captains' Dinner. This was agreed to and T. Cuneo was selected to paint it. Almost as soon as he started work, Dyer became seriously ill. He insisted on the continuance of the picture but died before his own portrait in the group was painted and it had to be completed from photographs. On his death bed he still remembered the cost of the picture and his solicitor arranged that the cost of £1000 be paid to the artist from his estate. There is an interesting minute of 25 August 1945: 'Letter from Mrs. Murray Brand, enclosing extract from Sotheby's catalogue describing the Club jugs and jars which were being offered for sale. Capt. Dyer attended the auction bought them and presented them to the Club. Efforts to discover how they left the Club's possession were unsuccessful.'

Bomb crater that destroyed the putting and driveway in World War II

Chapter 8 Royal Blackheath, during and after World War II

During the War the Clubhouse was occupied by the Home Guard, while Heath House was occupied by the Fire Brigade and the Air Raid Precautions Section. The course was once again grazed by sheep and, although golf was not banned, the course being in a neglected state and the shortage of golf balls severe, there was little golf played. Sundry bombs were dropped on the course, principally causing damage between the 7th and 12th fairways (damage which, subsequently, caused the Club to apply to the Crown for financial help in replacing trees). But a land mine, which dropped on the putting green immediately outside the front of the Clubhouse, caused much greater damage. The fact that the putting green was destroyed was not as important as the damage to the Clubhouse. On superficial examination this did not appear great but on inspection by experts revealed a gross weakening of the floor of the billiard room, bulging of the the outer walls and a large quantity of rotting timber. The Professional's cottage was also damaged. There is no record of any damage to Heath House, so one can assume that it escaped unscathed. Negotiations started with Messrs Clutton's, representing the Crown Agents, for the Landlord to carry out the necessary repairs. Negotiations were much protracted, owing, partly, to delays associated with the War Damage Commission and it was during this time that Bill Dyer, Captain of the Club and a well-known local Estate Agent, worked so hard and successfully that he not only persuaded the Crown Agents to make good all the damage but also to allow some of the interior of the house to be replanned, so as to make it more suitable for a Clubhouse (see p. 101). Dyer was authorised to sell Heath House for approximately £3,500 and he bought the cottage at the back for his two sisters for £1,000. The Crown Agents were asked to repair the damaged Professional's cottage and were subsequently asked to provide a bathroom also.

In 1947 Dyer, having prevailed upon the Crown Agents to allow some replanning of the inside of the house to make it more suitable as a Golf Clubhouse, set about the work and John Stevenson became an active partner in the project. In January 1952, it was suggested by Dyer that Heath House (which had not after all been sold) should be divided vertically into two houses and subsequently the two houses were sold for £5,142. By May 1954 the first stage of the repair/replanning had been completed but there remained much to be done. During 1955, while the work was continuing, furnishings, curtains and floor coverings were purchased. During this year also, the commanding officer

The team sent to Royal Montreal Golf Club (see p. 112)

Eltham Palace agreed to store the Club's valuable pictures during the restoration/repair work and arrangements were made for the pictures to be cleaned and restored also. In February 1956 a new lease of the Clubhouse and course was agreed with the Crown Agents and in March 1956 Dyer and Stevenson were able to report that all the replanning and restoration was complete, all refurnishing had been done and the cleaned and restored pictures returned to the Club from Eltham Palace.

In November 1956 Colonel Hoeck, immediate past-Captain of the Sundridge Park Golf Club, presented the Royal Blackheath Golf Club with some very old clubs used in the playing of chole.

On the catering side, also, there was some activity. In 1947 a large amount of crockery was bought to replace much that had been damaged or lost during the war. The food presented was not of great quality at this time: in 1948 the Blackheath Club of Sydney wrote to say that they had lodged with the Food for

Britain Fund names and addresses supplied to them by Royal Blackheath Golf Club and anticipated the arrival of food parcels in about three weeks' time.

In 1954 the House Committee reported to the AGM that the food at the Club had now improved 'now that food rationing had çeased' (So much for winning the War!).

The Course and Golf

During the period 1947–54 the Greens Committee actively pursued their purpose to restore the course. Trees were planted, drainage improved, re-turfing carried out. The Crown Agents were asked to repair the driveway. By October 1948 it was reported that the water pipes to 16 of the greens were working. Further extensive work to improve the course was planned in October 1949 by the Greens Committee. During 1952 it was found that although there were pipes to conduct the water to all the greens, the bore of the pipes was too small. Planning and work continued, funds permitting, and in March 1956 the Greens Committee were able to report that they had completed their plans to restore the course. The Committee had to appoint a warden in 1947 to prevent trespassers on the course: in July 1956 they put up notice boards to warn off trespassers, and members were advised to challenge anybody seen on the course who did not appear to be members. In March 1957 the Greens Committee had a discussion on the use of trolleys (a new development) on wet days.

During this time of replanning, refurnishing and reconstruction the Club also continued to play its matches and competitions. Some few matches were allowed to lapse but new matches were also introduced. At this time the Club consisted of 350 members in total and there was discussion as to whether this should now be regarded as a 'ceiling' because the course was getting overcrowded.

During the post-war period the Club had become more acutely aware of its importance in the historical golfing scene in England and of the need both to continue its traditions and to preserve its heritage. This showed itself in many ways, which at first sight are not apparently connected. W. F. Dyer–staunch traditionalist–bought back, at auction, at his own expense, the punch bowls and joram jars (see pp. 25–6) in 1945. In October 1948 the Royal College of Arms, in reply to a query from Royal Blackheath, stated that the arms of the Club were not registered and therefore were without authority. In 1952 the US Golf Association thanked the Club for the gift of one sleeve button and one coat button 'which have become part of an Exhibition at Golf House, New York'.

In June 1952 the Field Marshal, F. W. Farrington, wrote to the then Captain of the Club pointing out that this was the 150th anniversary year of the institution of the office of Field Marshal and that he wished to commemorate it by presenting a silver Captain's cleek to the Club. In the same year the match with the Edinburgh Burgess Golfing Society, first started in 1937 (a match in which both W. F. Dyer and Guy Eagleton played) because of the long tradition of co-operation and friendship between the Clubs (going back to Glennie or before) which had lapsed, was resurrected. In November 1952 the Duke of Edinburgh graciously agreed to extend his patronage to the Club and announced his intention, despite numerous other commitments, to take a personal interest in the Club. In November 1955, at a General Committee meeting, it was agreed to form an Historical Records Sub-committee 'to collate the Records of the Club from 1897 [the end of Hughes' *Chronicles*] with a view to putting the records in print, to form a continuation of Hughes' *Chronicles*. The original members of this Committee were: The Captain, the Immediate past-Captain, Brigadier F. Pocock, Bernard Parish and John Stevenson, with power to co-opt.

The 350th Anniversary

This active interest in the traditions of the Club and the whole reconstruction and replanning of both Clubhouse and course which had, as we know, been going on since 1947, had a final culmination in the preparations for the 350th Anniversary in 1958: the centenary of the winning of the great Foursomes Tournament by Glennie and Stewart came in 1957, but the celebration of this was left until 1958 so that the two events could be celebrated together. There was much bustle and activity in the preparation for this great landmark in the history of the Club. Several events were planned between 1 and 15 June. Committees of members planned and organised, while the loyal and willing Club staff put in many extra hours of work. The past-Captains' advice was sought as being those most steeped in the traditions of the Club. The principal competition was to be an Inter-Club Invitation Foursomes Tournament over 36 holes Medal Play on 15 June. Club teams were to consist of two players and it was possible for a Club to enter more than one team. Invitations to play were to be extended to all those Clubs that took part in the original Tournament plus all the Clubs both at home and abroad who had been particularly associated with Blackheath, and all their near neighbours in Kent.

In addition to this competition there was to be a match against Blackheath Football Club on 1 June and a match against Royal Calcutta Golf Club on 8 June. R. G. Hawkins compiled a short history of the Club for presentation to the competitors, for which he received the thanks of the Committee. There were to be Ladies' competitions and also Men's competitions. On the social side there was to be a Grand Dinner at the Park Lane Hotel: the trophies, Silver Clubs, etc., were all put on display in the Clubhouse.

During the same year the Committee recorded the following gifts:

1. The Field Marshal (F. W. Farrington) presented a fine carved oak chair to the Club to celebrate the 350th Anniversary and the Committee decided that it should be called the Farrington Chair.

2. Messrs W. E. B. Heliot and G. Young presented the Club with a fine and distinctive Notice Board incorporating an artistic reproduction of the ancient arms of the Club. This was erected at the entrance to the Club driveway on the North side while a smaller matching board was put up on the opposite side. Similar smaller boards were placed in front of the Clubhouse and on the 1st tee. The Committee expressed their thanks to these members and forwarded to each a copy of the minute recording their thanks.

3. A painting of the Clubhouse was presented by Mrs Aitken. The Secretary was directed to thank her, on behalf of the Committee.

4. The ultimate total for all the prizes was £296: the main prize was for the Inter-Club Foursomes and was a silver replica of the Claret Jug originally won by Glennie and Stewart. The Committee records that the price would have been much higher were it not for the generosity of a member, Mr Harry Vander, who supplied and engraved all the articles and whose firm also made the replica of the claret jug, all at a very favourable price.

The Foursomes Tournament was a great success: 74 teams entered from the following Clubs: Royal Blackheath, the Honorable Company of Edinburgh Golfers, the Royal and Ancient, Royal Calcutta, Royal Perth, Royal Burgess, Prestwick, Royal North Devon (Westward Ho!), Royal Musselburgh, Royal Wimbledon, Royal Liverpool, Royal Albert (Montrose), Dirleton Castle (East Lothian), North Berwick, Littlestone, Great Yarmouth and Caister, Formby, Royal Cinque Ports, Royal St George's, Walton Heath, Bruntsfield Links, Oxford University, London University, Cambridge University, West Hill, Royal Ashdown Forest, Sundridge Park, Maidstone, Langley Park, West Sussex, Woking, Worplesdon, Wentworth, Royal Dublin, Moor Park, Swinley Forest, Blackheath (Sydney, NSW), Berkhamstead, Knole Park, West Kent, Addington, Rochester and Cobham, Sidcup. The tournament was won by Wentworth, after a tie with Royal St George's, Wentworth having the best last round. As a fitting end to the 350th year celebrations there was a Grand Dinner at the Park Lane Hotel at which 400 people were present. The Captain in 1958 was F. M. Passmore.

The Club settled down after its great and successful 350th year celebrations and the next years were years of steady and continuous development. By 1961 the membership had risen to 623, an increase of 67 on the previous year but this resulting increase in income was more than offset by the steady erosive effect of inflation. The liquid assets of the Club were diminishing rapidly and its financial position became more dependent on the takings from the 'one-armed bandit' in the 19th-hole bar–£3,600 per annum. The Budget for the Greens Committee was £4,500 per annum and they had to abandon a scheme suggested by the golf architect, Mr Charles Hawtrey, for improving the 5th green, which for two years or more had been giving rise to much trouble (owing to inadequate drainage) because the cost was too high. It became a matter of urgency to fence the boundaries of the course because of ever-increasing vandalism and hooliganism and this was expensive. They appointed J. Woodin as Head Greenkeeper (from Langley Park) at a salary of £14 per week. In the fencing project and in other matters of course upkeep they came to an arragement with the Artisans, who agreed to provide help on the course as part of their duties as Artisan members, playing at a reduced subscription. At the same time the Greens Committee pointed out that there was only a half-trained man working on the course, other than the Head Greenkeeper and that the condition of the course was not likely to improve unless more men became available. In 1959 Sir Eric Savill of the Forestry Commission said that the Commission was willing to give the Club a quantity of trees and advise them also as to which type of tree should be planted in which part of the course. The Professional's Shop was to be improved and Thomas agreed to pay £100 towards the alterations.

In May 1959 the Field Marshal, F. W. Farrington, died and W. F. Dyer was elected Field Marshal. Matches continued to be played with enthusiasm and in March 1960 the Montrose Royal Albert Club arranged an invitation Inter-Club Foursomes Tournament to celebrate their 150th year. Blackheath were invited and decided to send four players and meet their travelling expenses. In 1961 R. G. Hawkins presented the King James Quaich for annual competition between the Royal Blackheath Golf Club and the Montrose Royal Albert Club. In 1961 Royal Blackheath sent a team to Bruntsfield Links Club for their bi-centenary anniversary celebrations.

Royal Blackheath continued to play all its traditional matches and to enter regularly in Kent Association competitions, London Foursomes, etc. Slight friction developed over the selection of the teams for the various matches. In the past it had always been done by the Match Committee inviting members individually: some members suggested that a list should be put on the noticeboard on which those who wished to play might put their names, the team to be selected from those names. No alteration in the method of team selection was made. A further mild but recurrent point of friction was that the General Committee were uneasy that the Captain was nominated by his predecessor, who had the advice of the past-Captains at the Captain's dinner and this nomination was expected to be supported by the General Committee. Some members of the Committee and some Club members objected to this 'rubber-stamping' and other methods were suggested: no change in the method of Captain selection was made.

In 1962 the portrait of the late Field Marshal, Farrington, was considered to be overcoloured and suggestions were made concerning the use of tinted glass to tone it down.

Because of continued rather poor numbers entering for the Boys' Medal, it was made an Open Competition for all the boys in Kent.

The Field Marshal, having already presented the Club with a Union Jack, now offered to pay any sum in excess of £50 required for the purchase of a new flagpole. In 1962 a portrait of Dyer was discussed: he would not allow this (see p. 102).

In 1966, W. Thomas, the Professional, was taken ill and decided, after recovery, to retire (see p. 113). George Johnson of the Lincoln Golf Club was appointed Professional.

In 1967 the House Committee decided that they must do interior decorating in the Clubhouse at a cost of between £1,500 and £2,500. They were asked to proceed with the work.

Further disagreement over team selection and Captain selection occurred. The former was partly solved by a (largely unwritten) agreement that the friendly matches would be organised by the Match Committee and would, in the main, be for friends in each Club who liked to play against one another, while the more official matches were selected from those who put their names on the Notice Board as being able and willing to play. The latter did not change, there being agreement that a traditional method of such antiquity should not be altered.

Brigadier W. Duncan of the Montrose Royal Albert Club was elected an Honorary Member of Royal Blackheath; his ancestor had been the first Captain of Blackheath.

In 1969 automatic watering was considered but found to involve a prohibitive expenditure. As a compromise, new plastic piping was installed to each green in such a manner as to allow of conversion to an automatic system at a later date.

In considering the internal redecorations the Committee agreed to the 'work-room' being redecorated and that it should become the Captain's Room–a room set aside for the Captain's and past-Captains' use, but which could be used by any member for luncheons, dinners, meetings, etc. when the Captains did not require it. The furnishings were to be provided by the Captains at their expense. There was much discussion on the need for the

Club to display all its trophies and treasures and on the question of security. It was finally agreed that steel display cabinets, with thick glass and special locks, would serve the purpose but there was little agreement as to the siting, and the cost was also much discussed.

In 1968 David Woolmer's score of 66 was recognised as a Course Record. The previous one of 67 had been made in 1965 by M. J. Curran.

In the same year the continuing work of the Historical Committee was considered. The Committee consisted of:

N. C. Clark   Chairman
The Field Marshal
F. A. W. Byron
Dr J. C. King
Commander J. I. T. Green

The Chairman asked for authority to purchase a British Museum Reader's ticket. Later in the same year Clark asked if the O'Shea room could be cleared temporarily to allow the Historical Committee to spread its documents. In 1969 the O'Shea room, a small room adjacent to both the Captain's room and the kitchen, had been cleared of much crockery and kitchen equipment and the possibility was considered of using it permanently as a meeting place and storeroom for the Historical Committee. By 1969 the room was being considered as the Club Library room. The question of the display cabinets was still being discussed and, in the course of listing and cataloguing the trophies it was found that a substantial number of trophies did not have the winner's name on them for several years. N. C. Clark and certain other members guaranteed £500–£600 toward the cost of the display cases.

The Club considered an Overseas Membership in view of the number of golfers abroad who had shown much interest in the Club.

In 1969 Dutch elm disease struck and the Secretary regretfully reported the felling of 126 elm trees. N. C. Clark aided the re-afforestation programme not only by giving young trees for planting but also by paying for the planting and protective staking.

In February 1970 serious consideration was given by the General Committee to raising the necessary funds to install an automatic watering system. It was decided to raise money:

(a) By a loan from the past-Captains' Fund
(b) By selling the reserve wine stock
(c) By reducing the reserves.

A great deal of further work was done on the course, mainly in the matter of drainage, as the course, being on clay, tended to get wet and boggy if there was much rain. At the same time it was felt by the Greens Committee that the layout of the course could be improved. A further worry to the Greens Committee was the continued necessary felling of trees affected by Dutch elm disease and the replacement of them. In all, 2,000 elm trees were lost and the cost of felling them was high. The automatic watering system was installed and, in 1972, appeared to be functioning satisfactorily, after various difficulties had been overcome, but there were doubts as to its continued efficiency and it was at least two years more of argument with the contractors before the system worked indeed satisfactorily.

The golf architect, Mr Frank Pennink, was asked to survey the whole course and to suggest improvements, in 1970. His suggestions were adopted and this resulted in the lengthening of the 5th, 10th, 13th and 15th holes. This was combined with a reshaping of the fairways by cutting the rough to make them narrower and also to give a dog-leg shape to as many holes as possible. Some 6–8 bunkers were to be grassed in and the planting of new trees to replace the elms was to be so arranged as not only to give a decorative effect but also to force the golfer to be more accurate.

The Artisans were granted permission to plant a tree by the 1st tee to commemorate the valuable services rendered by Wally Thomas to them over many years. Woodin, the Head Greenkeeper, coming to natural retirement, a new Head Greenkeeper was appointed and at the same time the Club bought a house, to be the Head Greenkeeper's house, in Sidcup.

On the golf and social side there was also activity. Guy Eagleton was elected Captain General (see p. 113). The Secretary reported that there were a growing number of good young golfers in the Club, which was encouraging as there had been a lack of such young men for some years. The trend was encouraged by the Club. In 1973 they suggested that the Juniors formed their own Committee and ran their own affairs, within the general framework of the Club. The Boys' Medal, originally for Blackheath boys only, and the oldest boys' competition in England, now open to all the youthful golfers of Kent, was flourishing and had a regular entry of 40–50.

The total number of members now exceeded 600, there being 329 male full-playing members and 98 lady full-playing members. It was decided that the ceiling should be 325 male full-playing members and 100 lady full-playing members. This meant the operation of a Waiting List and the Club, in 1973, formed an Interviewing Committee to ensure that new members should be of 'the right type'.

The friendly and official matches continued: in 1972, spurred on by the then Captain, Donald Tindley, the Club decided to send a team of four to the Centenary Celebrations of the Royal Montreal Golf Club and they took with them a Silver Quaich, suitably inscribed, as a memento of the Centenary. The Quaich was presented by Royal Blackheath Golf Club. Guy Eagleton, aged 80, accompanied the team (see p. 104).

In March 1970 the House Committee entertained a new concept of the O'Shea room, i.e. that it should become an Historical Museum and Library and that the display cases for the trophies should be in that room, where they could be on view for those who wanted to see them and in which site security would be better than in the Entrance Hall–the other suggested site. This matter was agreed and N. C. Clark began to organise matters.

In July 1970 it was reported to the Committee that Mr W. Patterson had had the beautiful oil 'Golf on Blackheath 1875' cleaned and restored at his own expense and for this the Committee expressed its gratitude on behalf of the Club.

The Committee decided to have Wally Thomas's portrait painted: due to his illness, leading to his death, much of the portrait had to be done from photographs. It was duly completed (and is considered to be a good likeness) and hangs in the Mixed Lounge.

In September 1973 the Museum and Library, complete with secure display cases containing all the trophies and silver clubs, was opened: a very fitting room for a Club which has a great past and an ever active interest in the traditions of golf today.

The Eagleton Family

1 *John T. Eagleton* (1860–1942)
John Eagleton was born in Blackheath and was a founder member of Eltham Golf Club; he was Captain of Royal Blackheath Golf Club in 1925 (after the amalgamation). After he left school he went into the Law, being articled to his father O. C. T. Eagleton, who was a solicitor in Blackheath. He subsequently went into partnership with his father. He was a most capable administrator and this ability, added to the fact the he was a close friend of Christian Gray, had much to do with the successful amalgamation of the two Clubs, as has been already pointed out. Not only was he a golfer but he was also a good cricketer and an active member of Eltham Cricket Club; he was present at an Eltham match in 1914 when his two sons, Hugh and Guy, played in a match in which Dr W. G. Grace (who was also a resident of Eltham) played his last game of cricket, making 69 not out.

2 *Guy T. Eagleton* (son of John Eagleton)
Guy Eagleton joined Eltham Golf Club in 1922 and subsequently, in 1925, became a Royal Blackheath member. He was a fine golfer and won not only the Spring Medal but also many other scratch and handicap trophies. He was a contemporary (and

John Eagleton

Guy Eagleton being congratulated by the Captain, Donald Tindley, on his election as Captain General.

great friend) of W. F. Dyer and, with the latter, played a most active part in reviving the fortunes of the Club after World War II. At the time of Dyer's death, Guy Eagleton was offered the honour of Field Marshal but had to decline as he lived rather far away from Blackheath and felt he could not properly carry out the Field Marshal's duties from his home. In 1973, in his 80th year, he expressed a wish to accompany the then Captain, Donald Tindley, and the team of past-Captains to Montreal, Canada, for the Centennial Celebrations of the Royal Montreal Golf Club and made the tour with them. In the same year, the past-Captains decided to honour him for his long and devoted service to the Club by bestowing the title of Captain General upon him: he being only the second holder of that title since Henry Callender in 1807.

Walter Thomas (1896–1973)

'Wally' Thomas, as the Club knew him, was born in 1896. As a youth he was assistant to Ernest Jones at Chislehurst. Jones emigrated to America in the early 1920s and, when he left, Wally went as Professional to Braeside, a private Golf Club in the Beckenham area. From Braeside he got an appointment as Assistant Professional to Reith at Royal Blackheath Golf Club in 1922. When Reith retired, Wally became Professional and remained at Blackheath until 1966 when, having completed 44 years' service to the Club, he retired at 70 years of age.

He was a fine striker of the ball, but a poor short putter. In particular, his iron play was much admired and many of his brother professionals came to him for advice in this particular department. In later life, poor eyesight made golf difficult for him. An enthusiast for 'high hands' in the backswing, he was a patient and kindly teacher with a good gift of communication. Those who knew him well describe him as a charming, kindly

Wally Thomas

Paddy Connolly

man but a poor business man, owing to his tendency to give things away and his willingness to do many small jobs for little or nothing. He was of middle height and in his later years a little portly. He always played golf in a trilby hat and wore a collar and tie.

His wife was as delightful and charming as he was: she survives him. They had one son, Roger, who was assistant to his father and then became Professional at Pyle and Glenfig Club in South Wales. It is a measure of the loyalty that Royal Blackheath inspires, that Wally's son regularly attends the Annual Dinner and keeps in touch with some of the members.

Wally was a good friend to the Artisans, helping them in many ways and usually accepting little or no money for his services. When he retired in September 1966 he received a testimonial and a cheque for £1,228; he was also given a gold watch worth £50 by the Club and the Ladies' Section gave him a table lamp. Mrs Thomas was given a present, also valued at £50.

In addition, arrangements were made to have his portrait painted and he was made an Honorary Life Members. After he retired he continued to play at Blackheath, though his health and eyesight were failing; he was given a handicap of 8. It was his ambition to win one of the major Club trophies but this he never achieved, though he did win the Queen Victoria Diamond

George Johnson

Jubilee Cup (matchplay handicap). By the time arrangements had been made for the painting of his portrait he was a sick man and the portrait was completed after his death, having been mainly done from a number of photographs. It hangs in the Mixed Lounge and was painted by Mr Nockels, who was a member of Royal Blackheath. Wally Thomas died in September 1973.

George Johnson
(1911–)

The present professional, George Johnson, was appointed in 1966. He was born in Torksey, Lincolnshire and became assistant to the local Club professional in his teens. He first became a full Professional at Rivervale, Sheffield, in 1932; subsequently he was Professional at Bulwell Forest, Nottingham and at Sherwood Forest. Prior to coming to Blackheath, he was at South Staffs, Wolverhampton for 14½ years. He has been a player of considerable ability, winning the Notts Championship on 6 consecutive occasions and being Runner-up in the Midland Championship fourteen times. In 1952 he reached the semi-Final of the News of the World Match Play Championship. In fact, he did so well in many tournaments that, if the present tournament points system had been in operation when he was at his best, he would have been a sure choice for the Ryder Cup.

Clearly, as an assistant, he was well grounded in the art of clubmaking and he has continued to practice the art all his life, making, in particular, beautiful wooden putters.

He has two sons who are both golf professionals and continue the family tradition.

During his time at Blackheath he has been a true Club professional, a most worthy successor to the long line of Blackheath professionals before him.

'Paddy' Connolly
(1921–)

Paddy was appointed Assistant Steward in July 1939, and is still in the service of the Club. He was born at Longford, Ireland, on 4 December 1921. His father served in the British Army in World War I and subsequently served in the Irish Army; he had been wounded in World War I and this affected his health afterwards. By 1930 Paddy and his sister had lost both their parents.

The British Legion stepped in to help both of them in their education and, in the later thirties, Paddy went to the Nautical School of Cookery in London. This school was run by Commander Lauder RN. Lauder was a member of Royal Blackheath and he suggested in July 1939 that Paddy should become Assistant Steward at Royal Blackheath. Paddy remained at Blackheath until 1941 when he joined up (in the RAF) and was demobilised in 1946. Up to 1941 he lived in the wine cellar at the Club: the ground floor and basement floor being in use by the Home Guard and the upper floors closed off. It was during this time that the land mine was dropped on the drive outside the front of the Clubhouse. Paddy recalls that it was a delayed-action mine and that a mild thump signalled its arrival; he spent a cold and very uncomfortable night (in pyjamas and greatcoat) in a pillbox at the back of the Clubhouse. The bomb went off on the following morning and 'the whole clubhouse rose up about 1½ inches and fell back'.

During the war the Club's pictures were stored in one of the Haberdasher Company's Schools in South Wales. When demobbed in 1946 he had three months' leave due but within three weeks he became bored and returned to the Club as Steward. He remembers the discomforts of the reconstruction period 1951–56, when so much of the Clubhouse was out of action; during much of this time he lived in his upstairs flat (accompanied at this time by his wife Ellen whom he had married in 1948) and had to climb down a scaffolding catwalk with a rope rail to get to his work. He saw the Club through these difficult times, aided by his wife, who was Assistant Stewardess and Catering Manageress, and they have remained ever since. Paddy plays golf (occasionally now because he is too busy) and at one time had a handicap of 7. He presides at the 19th hole and keeps the bets and fines books.

For many years he has been a keen supporter of the Golf Stewards' Golfing Society and has been elected Chairman on two occasions.

Because of his long experience and love for the Club, he is more knowledgeable on the traditions and customs of the Club than any member and has a major role to play at the Annual Dinner, at which he is responsible for the Silver Club, which is part of the Captain's initiation ceremony and he, in particular, is the man who knows the proper position of all the trophies on the table. He is also well able to see to it that a 'Wee Dinner' is properly conducted and has been known to point out the error of his ways to any member present who is not well versed in tradition.

Paddy has now completed 41 years' service to the Club: his good humour and fund of reminiscence (the latter recounted in an Irish accent he has never lost) allied to a hard-working efficiency and an ability never to forget a face, make him a well-loved and trusted servant of the Club.

Brigadier F. Pocock MC, OBE (1896–)

Brigadier Pocock was born at Bridgewater in 1896.

As a boy he was a keen Scout and became a Silver Wolf, this award being the highest possible award in Scouting and made by nomination of fellow Scouts.

At 10 years of age he joined the 5th Volunteer Battalion of the Somerset Light Infantry, as a bugler; on the formation of the Territorial Army in 1908 he joined the West Somerset Yeomanry, as a bugler, and subsequently played the bugle before

King Edward VII.

He served in World War I and gained the Military Cross. During peacetime he served with the Royal Artillery; he is a man of intellect and invention; these qualities he put to good use in his life. He gained a BSc of London University, in mathematics and physics: his inventiveness and scientific mind caused him to make a number of improvements to guns and in World War II he was the first man in the Ministry of Supply to be awarded the Order of the British Empire.

He is a Fellow of the Physical Society and a Companion of the Institute of Mechanical Engineers.

During his service at the Military College of Science he was successful in the examination for the Past Advanced Class at that College, a class which made a special study of artillery problems.

In more recent years he has become a Member of the Institute for the Measurement of Movement and Control, an Institute largely concerned with the new science of Cybernetics and he remains an active member.

He first played golf at Royal Blackheath in 1923 when, as an Army Officer, he could play for a shilling a day. He never played on the old Heath course. He joined Royal Blackheath in 1948 and has lived in Blackheath ever since. He subsequently became Captain of Blackheath in 1951 and was elected Field Marshal in 1974. He was a founder member of the Historical Committee and even when no longer a member he continued to give vigorous support to the aims of the Committee, being a firm believer in the historical importance of Royal Blackheath in the great tradition of golf.

A kindly, open-hearted man, he is, in no small part, responsible both for the continued and enthusiastic work of the Historical Committee, whose researches have done much to provide a basis for this book, and for the decision of the Committee and the Royal Blackheath Golf Club to publish it.

Blackheath and Ladies' Golf

Blackheath, traditionally, is a men's Club and, during the time that they played on the Heath, women did not play on the course. In 1906 F. S. Ireland suggested that they might be permitted to attend a Buffet at the Club and see the trophies, but the Committee deferred decision on this.

Christian Gray's wife was a golfer and, it is said, sought the right of ladies to play. Gray bought land at Barnehurst, a short distance away, and helped them to make a course on it. The Blackheath Ladies' Golf Club was founded in December 1899, having a Clubhouse at No. 3 Montpelier Row. This was a ladies' Club exclusively and when he died in 1932 the ladies of Blackheath (the amalgamation with Eltham having taken place in 1923) raised a subscription for a memorial to him. The memorial took the form of an electric clock which was installed in the Mixed Lounge in 1933. Thus, the ladies had no connection with Royal Blackheath until the amalgamation with Eltham in 1923/4 when they joined in with the Ladies' Section of Eltham Golf Club. In 1923 the Secretary of the Ladies' Club at Barnhurst offered the Club's Silver Cup and Medal (one of the cups presented by C. H. Gray) for Annual Competition by the Blackheath Ladies' Club at Eltham. By 1921–2 the Barnhurst course had fallen into such a poor state that golf was no longer possible there. Thus the move to Eltham came at a very providential time. A Golf Club still exists at Barnehurst but is now a mixed Club. In October 1923 an Extraordinary General Meeting was called to approve new Rules and Regulations for the Blackheath Ladies' Golf Club at Eltham.

The ladies have continued to play at Eltham ever since and Ladies' Competitions took place during the 350th year celebrations. Their numbers are limited to 100 and they have their own Club Office in the main building, but as far as the rest of the Clubhouse is concerned, they have the use of their own changing rooms, the Mixed Lounge and the Dining Room only.

Caricature of some members of Royal Blackheath Golf Club by Syd Jordan, 1956

Chapter 9 The golf balls and clubs

No history of Blackheath can be written without some explanation of the part played by the golf ball, because the great development of the game of golf can be directly attributed to the wonderful strides made in perfecting the ball and making golf a more pleasant game to play. Furthermore, there is no doubt that Blackheath itself played a leading role in the introduction of the first rubber–or gutta–ball, in 1848, although the very nature of the Club minutes, concerned as they were with formal matters, prevented any observations on golf balls throughout its history.

To those unfamiliar with the history of the game, it should be explained that the ball in use up until the middle of the nineteenth century, was what was known as a 'feathery'. This was a leather ball, stuffed with feathers, first described in a famous poem 'The Goff' by Thomas Mathison (1744):

> '. . . the work of Bobson; who with matchless art
> Shapes the firm hide, connecting every part,
> Then in a socket sets the well-stitched void
> And thro' the eyelet drives the downy tide;
> Crowds urging crowds the forceful brogue impels,
> The feathers harden and the Leather swells; . . .'

In appearance they were not unlike the modern Fives ball.

Although, as has been seen, Blackheath had its own club-makers prior to 1800, no evidence has been found that they ever had their own feather ballmakers. They must have obtained their supplies either from St Andrews or from Edinburgh. These balls were expensive. A man could only make three or four a day and they cost from 2s 6d to 4s. They flew well in dry weather, but when they got wet they wheezed through the air. Above all they were mortally afflicted if badly struck by an iron club, when they would disintegrate. There are two very large feathery balls in the Blackheath showcase, they have been dated 1735, but it is impossible to confirm these dates.

The most important development in the history of golf was the use of rubber in the making of a ball. What was known as rubber came originally from Brazil, and by the 1820s Hancock and Macintosh had already discovered its waterproofing abilities. In 1838 Queen Victoria had given her dog 'Dash' three rubber balls for Christmas and by the same year Hancock and Goodyear of the USA had discovered how to vulcanise or harden the rubber ball by the use of sulphur. Someone may well have tried to use it for making a golf ball, but as it had the qualities of what we now

Hand-hammered gutta

know as India rubber, it probably bounced too much.

The position changed dramatically with the discovery in 1843 of an entirely different 'gum' called 'gutta percha' (tree-sap) in Malaya by Mr William Montgomerie, a surgeon of the East India Company. He found in his travels in Malaya, that the handles of knives, whips and hoes were made of a hard substance, which could however be softened by immersion in hot water. He sent specimens to London stating the uses to which the material might be put, including the making of medical vessels. He received the gold medal of the Society for the Encouragement of Arts Manufactures and Commerce in June 1845.

The arrival of the first gutta percha golf ball in 1848 was not well chronicled at the time and the only contemporary account was in the form of the song 'In Praise of Gutta Percha', sung by its writer, W. Graham of Edinburgh, at the Autumn Meeting of the Innerleven Golf Club, Fife, on 1 September 1848. (See Appendix I of *Golf in the Making* 1979, p. 317). There was however another reference in James Balfour's *Reminiscences of Golf at St. Andrews Links* (Edinburgh 1887), which has direct reference to Blackheath, as follows:

> 'About the beginning of the year 1848 balls were made of Gutta Percha. I remember the commencement perfectly. My brother-in-law Admiral Maitland Dougal played a doubles match at Blackheath with the late Sir Ralph Anstruther and William Adam of Blair Adam and another friend with gutta percha balls on a very wet day. They afterwards dined together at Sir Charles Adams' at Greenwich Hospital and Sir Ralph said after dinner "A most curious thing–here is a golf ball of gutta-percha; Maitland and I have played with it all day in the rain and it flies better at the end of the day than it did at the beginning". Maitland came to Edinburgh immediately after and told me of this. We at once wrote to London for some of these balls and went to Musselburgh to try them. Gourlay the ball maker had heard of them and followed us on round. . . . He was alarmed.'

Sir Thomas Montcrieffe

Thus we know that someone at Blackheath was then making the new balls, which were immediately ordered by James Balfour and his brother-in-law Sir Maitland Dougal and played with at Musselburgh, Gourlay, the feather ballmaker, being a more than interested spectator. We also know that a Blackheath member, Sir Thomas Moncrieffe, sent some sheet gutta percha to Willie Dunn at Musselburgh (the latter was trained in the first place by Gourlay as a feather ballmaker) to make some balls. This is how we know that in 1848 someone was making them at Blackheath and it seems as logical a place as any for this to happen. Amongst

Ten Silver King golf balls in a case

Half a Century of Golf Ball Development

The balls in the case below are reproductions of Golf Balls produced by the Silvertown Company since 1888, and are identical with the types of ball driven off at a demonstration held on the Company's testing ground at Barnehurst Golf Club (Kent) on 27th July, 1932.

Three balls of each type were driven from a driving machine, the impulse to which was derived from the action of gravity on a 600 lb. weight. The machine was set uniformly throughout the test to a drive equivalent to that of a first-class player. The Human Element was provided by Leonard Bates, the Club Professional. The weather during the test was fine with an intermittent following wind.

The demonstration was given to show the increase in length due to modern methods of construction whilst the smooth ball (J) shows by contrast the effect of the marking on a ball. The distances driven are shown below in yards.

CODE	NAME	DATE USED	WGT. DWTS	DIAMETER	L. BATES		MACHINE*	
					Carry	Run	Average Carry	Run
	GUTTIES							
A	Silvertown No. 4—27½	1888	27½	1.73 inch	165	182	174	206
B	Silvertown No. 4 Remade	1888	25	1.68 ,,	165	186	164	185
C	Silvertown No. 4—28	1890	28	1.76 ,,	150	183	177	197
D	Silvertown No. 5—28	1898	28	1.76 ,,	157	189	175	195
E	Bramble	1900	25	1.68 ,,	180	197	191	216
	RUBBER CORED							
F	Silver King Black Dot Mesh	1913-1922	31	1.645 ,,	208	241	220	259
G	King Plus	1932	29½	1.62 (1.62" × 1.62 oz. nominal)	220	270	244	271
H	Silver King U.S.G.A. size	1930	28¼	1.68 (1.68" × 1.55 oz. nominal)	224	231	242	269
I	Silver King U.S.G.A. size	1932	29½	1.68 (1.68" × 1.62 oz. nominal)	230	261	244	278
J	This is a rubber-cored golf ball made to Silver King present day specification 1.62 diam., but with plain surface				95	105	111	147

*Average of 3 shots

its members were City merchants connected with the Far East and they must have been fully aware of the possibilities presented by this new material.

There was in fact another circumstance, which may have been coincidental, and that was the presence at Woolwich of the rubber manufactory of S. W. Silver, the tropical-kit manufacturers in the City. In 1852 it moved across the river to create Silvertown and became the future home of the India Rubber Works and Telegraph Company. Thirty years later they did make golf balls, the extremely hard Silvertown No. 4, which introduced the gutty as opposed to the pure gutta percha ball–the gutta. Later they are remembered as the creators of the famous Silver King ball and because of the close connection the company had with the Club through its one-time chairman Christian Gray and his family.

In 1851 Willie Dunn was appointed 'Keeper of the Green' at Blackheath and made guttas under the trade name of 'Dunn of London'. It says something for his reputation that the Royal Burgess Company record the purchase of his balls from London.

The gutta balls now being used were easy to make and above all were cheap–selling for 1s each. What is more, they could last for ever if you did not lose them. They were made at first by heating the substance in hot water, and rolling by hand, and were then allowed to cool in cold water, when they hardened. Later, moulds were used. The first balls were smooth and would not fly properly until they had been hacked. This fault was rectified by hand-hammering. The greatest defect was that they would not take paint properly and surviving examples are black or yellow-brown in colour and must have been difficult to find. Paint was to be a problem into the twentieth century, when new and better types became available.

It is still necessary to follow the development of the ball because of its effect upon the enjoyment of the game. The 'gutta' was a cheap ball and more players could afford the game, but by the 1880s the 'gutty' or hard composite ball was appearing and having a decisive effect on the design of wooden clubs. Those beautiful long heads were being smashed to pieces by the hard ball. This also encouraged the greater use of iron clubs.

Then out of the blue came the next great development in the game of golf–the arrival from the USA of the Haskell core-wound ball. This at once made the game easier and more pleasant to play. The ball flew a further 25 yards or so and, even when mis-hit, the results were not so disastrous. This ball was relatively expensive and cost 2s 6d, when iron clubs were 3s 6d and woods 5s, but it did not matter–the improvement was so decisive. It also affected every golf course, all of them in the end having to be lengthened to accommodate the new ball. Far-sighted members of Blackheath had by then already sensed that the day would come when a move from Blackheath would become essential. In spite of every effort to make a competitive solid ball, the principle of a core-wound ball still rules supreme today–at a cheaper price than ever before in relation to clubs.

Today's members of the Royal Blackheath Golf Club may feel that some or other of their past members played a significant part in the development of the game some 130 years ago and that this should rightly be added to their traditions.

Wooden Clubs

Prior to 1848, when the 'feathery' ball was in use, golf clubs had wooden heads. A single iron club might be in the player's bag for use in really difficult situations or when conditions were such that a wooden club might be broken in attempting the shot.

The main reason for this was because the feather ball could easily be burst by an iron club and at that time balls were more expensive than clubs.

Until about 1900, the wooden shaft was attached to the beechwood head of the club by a long splice, a type of joint used in the mending of ship's spars and masts, called a 'scarffed' joint. In the golf clubmakers' workshop it became known as a 'scared' joint and such clubs are often referred to as 'scared-head' clubs.

The heads of these clubs, prior to 1885, were long and slender and the face of the club had a well-marked concave appearance, often referred to as 'hook-faced'. The club was balanced and weighted by pouring melted lead into a cavity at the back and the lower edge of the face of the club was reinforced by the insertion of a strip of ram's horn. The shafts were of ash, until the mid 1820s when hickory was used, and were approximately 43 inches long in the longer clubs. The leather grips were much thicker than those of a modern club, having an underlay or rind of strips of cloth.

After 1848, the gutta percha ball appeared.

The gutta ball, being hard, damaged the club faces and many of the club faces were repaired with vulcanite, leather or horn inserts.

In 1885, the shape of club heads made a dramatic change: the heads became shorter and the faces were deeper and convex instead of concave. Drivers of this type came to be known as 'Bulger' drivers. By 1900, persimmon wood began to be imported in large quantities from the USA for making club heads, as it had much better qualities than beechwood. At about the same time, the scared joint was abandoned and the shaft was fitted into a hole in the wooden club head. This form of socket joint, still in use, caused these clubs to be known as socket-headed clubs.

Types of wooden club in the first half of the nineteenth century

Driver	used from the tee
Grassed Driver	used from a good fairway lie
Long Spoon	used from a poor fairway lie
Middle Spoon } Short Spoon } Baffing Spoon }	all with varying degrees of loft and used mainly for hitting a high shot on to the green
Wooden Niblick	used for hitting the ball out of small holes
Wooden Putter	used on the putting green and for running shots to the green.

Exhibition case containing 13 clubs and 2 feather balls (the club on the right is shown in the portrait of Henry Callender (see p. 18))

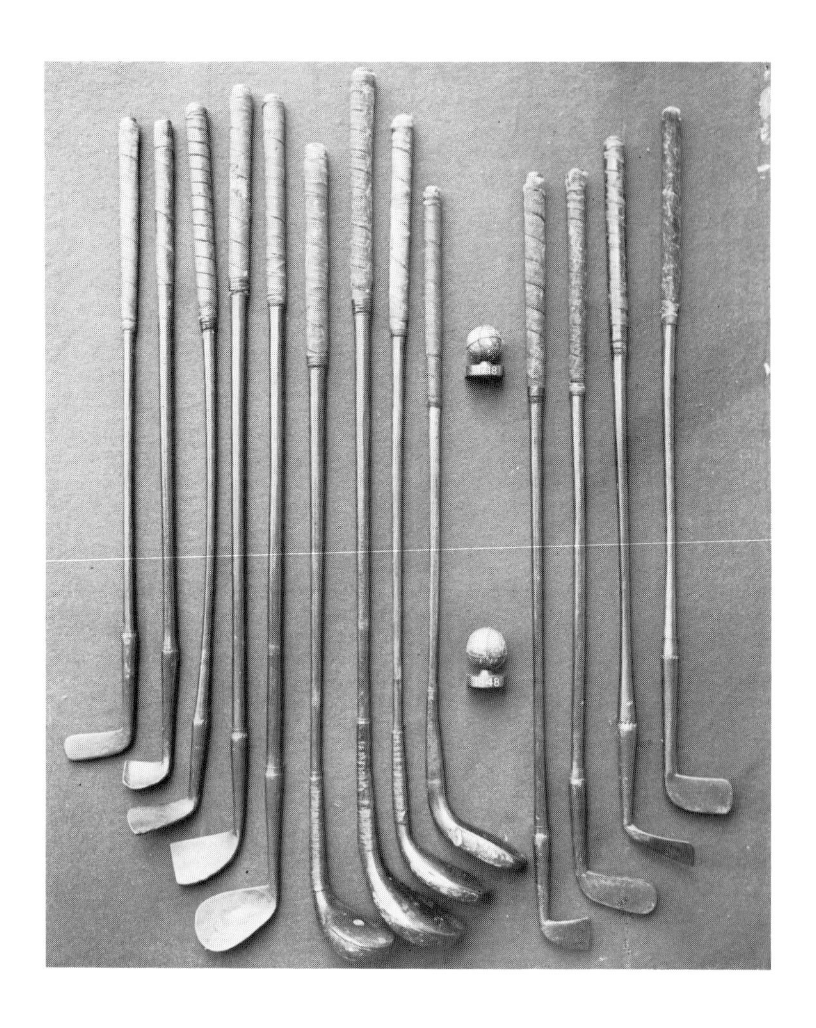

Wooden clubs in use in the latter half of the nineteenth century and up to World War I

Driver	used from the tee
Brassie	somewhat like a wooden niblick: the sole of the club brass shod to prevent damage when playing off a hard surface.
Spoon	used for playing out of poor lies
Wooden Niblick	up to about 1895
Putter	by 1900 iron putter blades were coming into fashion.

In the early part of the twentieth century wooden club heads became small. After World War I, the heads became larger. In the late 1920s hollow steel shafts were introduced and the hickory shaft disappeared.

Iron Clubs

As has been said, before 1848 a player's bag would likely contain one iron club: this club was used from very bad lies and was something of a last resort. It was often of use in getting the ball out of ruts, cart tracks and from places where the ball was among stones.

Wooden clubmakers were experts in wood but not in metalwork. They therefore turned to the blacksmiths to get the iron club head made: the iron head had a socket into which the wooden shaft was fitted by the wooden clubmaker, being held there by a rivet. The wooden clubmaker also put a leather grip on the club.

The early iron club heads were hammered out on an anvil by a blacksmith and were fairly crude affairs. After 1850, when the gutta ball appeared, a ball which did not disintegrate as easily as the feathery, more iron clubs appeared in the golfer's bag and by the end of the century there were more iron clubs than wooden clubs in a golf bag. By this time not only were there more iron clubs but many more golfers. Blacksmiths with an aptitude for shaping iron club heads found full employment at it and became full time 'cleekmakers', with a number of apprentices. By the early twentieth century, drop forging was being used to produce iron club heads and this allowed mass production methods to be used to produce thousands of heads each exactly the same.

Types of iron club before 1850

Rutter, or Track Iron	A very early iron club, it had a small and heavy head being designed to fit into ruts and cart tracks.
General Purpose Iron	Also an early iron club: heavy, well lofted and the face concave but longer than the rutter.

Types of iron club 1850–1885

Cleek	A shallow-faced iron used for hitting long iron shots.
Lofting Iron	A development from the General Purpose iron.
The Iron Niblick	This was a well-lofted iron with a face larger than a rutter, used for bunker play as well as bad lies and also for high stopping approach shots.

General observations on the Blackheath clubs

Antique wooden and iron clubs in this collection are very old. At least three of the wooden clubs can be dated as before 1830. Of the slightly later clubs the Tom Morris putter is a good example of his work and the two drivers by Bob Kirk are most beautiful clubs and in a remarkable state of preservation. The iron clubs are as old as any in existence and are more numerous than in any other collection. They exhibit all the characteristics of really old irons with heavy heads, large hoses, dished faces, blacksmith's hammer marks and many are of the 'cut-off' nose type.

This uniquely large and old collection of irons must give rise to some speculation. Why such a high proportion, in the entire collection, of irons to woods? It may be coincidence but this is very unlikely; a much more likely explanation is the terrain over which golf was played at Blackheath. This was a very rough, tough course and moreover played between gravel pits: much as the player wished to avoid them there must have been many shots played out of them. It is likely, also, that if there was so much gravel in the subsoil, there must also have been many stones on the surface of the course. All of this adds up to the fact that wooden clubs could easily be damaged and therefore, despite the possible dangers to the feathery ball incurred in using iron clubs, they had to be used more frequently than they would have been on a sandy, links, seaside course.

The bets books contain many examples of matches played with iron clubs only.

A question that also springs to mind is, where were these iron clubs made? They may have all been imported from Scotland, but a more likely explanation is that Donaldson and those before and after him up to about 1850 found a local blacksmith and instructed him as to what sort of head to make, afterwards fitting a shaft and grip. We know that there were a number of blacksmith's shops in the vicinity of the Green Man Public House in Blackheath.

The Blackheath clubs and balls

Clubs

In showcases on the walls in the hall and in the Museum are 25 clubs used in playing golf, 6 'Ceremonial' clubs with silver balls attached to the shaft and 6 miniature clubs and 12 balls.

Balls

2 feathery golf balls and 17 gutta and gutty golf balls. The distinction between the two is that the gutta (earlier) ball is of pure gutta percha whereas the gutty (later) ball is a composite ball composed of gutta percha and various agents to make it harder and less disposed to disintegrate. 10 Silver King rubbercore balls in a special display case.

Clubs used in play

1 *Wooden clubs*

(a) Driving Putter circa 1835. Maker unknown. A scared-head club with a big splice. Very thick whipping on the scare. A rounded area on the top of the head looks to have held a disc, now missing, probably with the maker's name.

Driving putter: Long spoon:
Baffing spoon

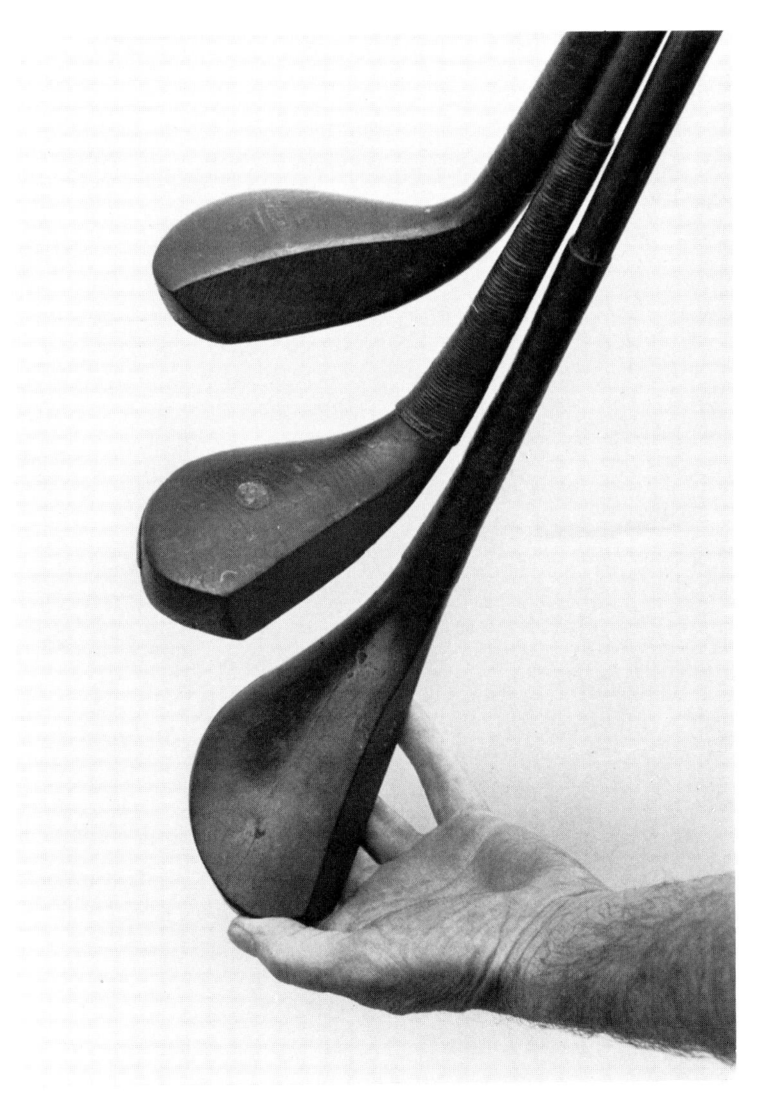

Length: 38″
Head Length 5″
Width $2\frac{1}{4}$″ Weight $1\frac{1}{3}$ lbs.
Depth $1\frac{1}{4}$″
Grip: Sheepskin, good condition

(b) Long spoon circa 1820. Maker unknown. A lofted wooden club with a very big splice and a markedly hooked face. The shaft is thick and probably of ash.

Length: 41″
Head: Length $5\frac{1}{4}$″
Width $2\frac{3}{4}$″ Weight $1\frac{1}{4}$ lbs.
Depth $1\frac{1}{4}$″
Grip: Sheepskin, good condition

(c) Baffing spoon, circa 1850, by Ludovic Sandison, Aberdeen (1825–1884). A well-lofted scared-head wooden club. The shaft is of hickory. The leather grip is in good condition. The face of the club has a definite hooked appearance. Initials on the head 'C.A.' are probably those of the owner.

Length: $37\frac{1}{2}''$
Head: Length $4\frac{3}{4}''$
Width $2\frac{1}{2}''$ Weight $1\frac{1}{4}$ lbs.
Depth 1.1/6″

(d) Wooden putter circa 1850 by Tom Morris, St Andrews (1821–1906). A scared-head club with a straight face.

Length: 23″
Head: Length 5″
Width $1\frac{3}{4}''$ Weight $\frac{3}{4}$ lb.
Depth 1″
Grip: Sheepskin

(e) and (f) Two drivers circa 1875 by Bob Kirk of St Andrews (1845–1886) and also professional at Blackheath 1864–1866. Scared-head clubs. The faces of these clubs are only slightly hooked. They are beautifully made and finished. The grips are in excellent condition: it is possible that these clubs have not been used.

Length: 41″
Head: Length $4\frac{3}{4}''$
Width $2\frac{1}{2}''$ Weight 1 lb.
Depth $1\frac{1}{4}''$

(g) Middle spoon circa 1855 by Tom Morris, St Andrews (1821–1906) A scared-head club.

Length: 41″
Head: Length 5″ Face hooked.
Width 2″ Weight 1 lb.
Depth $1\frac{1}{4}''$ Good sheepskin grip.

(h) Driver circa 1880 by W. Campbell (1862–1900) A scared-head club with good sheepskin leather grip.

Length: $43\frac{1}{2}''$
Head: Length $4\frac{3}{4}''$
Width $1\frac{3}{4}''$
Depth $1\frac{1}{4}''$

Spoon circa 1925 by R. J. Gibson of Westward Ho! (B. 1888). Professional at Royal Calcutta 1921–1948. Socket-headed, good condition.

Length: 40″

Miniature golf clubs and gutta balls

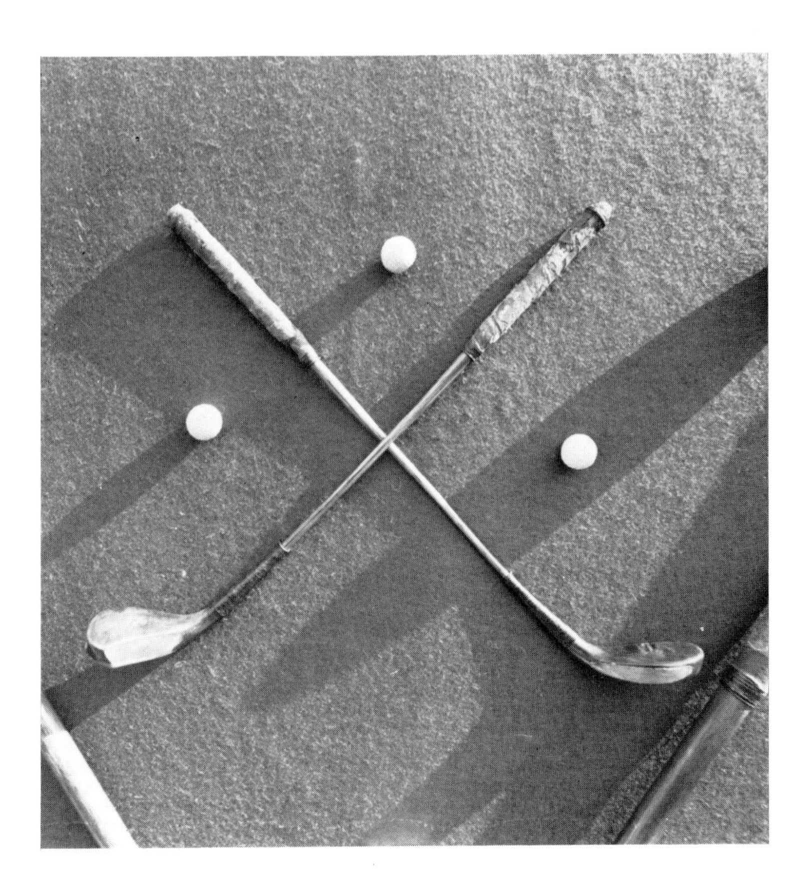

(j) Bull Dog Brassie circa 1920 by the Sundridge Park professional. A socket-headed club with the typical deeply convex brass-shod sole of such clubs.
Length: 42″

2 *Aluminium-headed club* by Willie Dunn Jr of North Berwick (1865–1952). Date unknown, probably between 1910 and 1922. Marked 'Patent applied for'. The club, two-faced, is 45″ long. On the righthand side, there is an extra metal face with vulcanite behind it and so little loft as to suggest that it is a driver. On the lefthand side the face has a definite loft and no extra facing. Depth of each face approximately 1″. The shaft is inserted into the aluminium head socket and carried right through to appear at the sole. (That part in the socket is oval in cross-section).

3 *Iron clubs*

(a) Straight-faced iron, probably a putter, date unknown but probably before 1840. A heavy club, the head blacksmith-made. The hose is large in diameter and with coarse knurling at the top. Weight 1 lb. Large shaft, probably hickory. Sheepskin grip. No maker's mark on head.

Case showing miniature clubs and 12 miniature golf balls, two wooden clubs by R. Kirk and 12 gutta balls made by Kirk

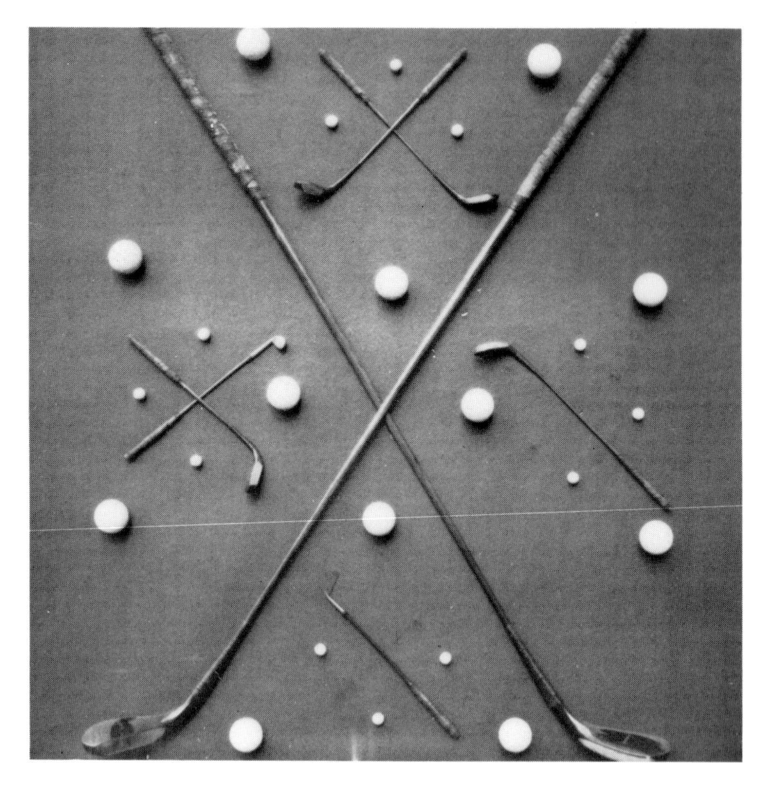

Length: 31″
Hose: 5″
Face: Length 4″
Depth $1\frac{1}{4}$″

(b) Rutter or Rut-iron with 'cut-off' nose. No maker's name. Probably blacksmith-made before 1800. A heavy club with a well-hooked, and dished face. A big hose and a thick shaft which may be ash. Hose, coarse, knurling at the top. The under grip only is present.

Length: 33″
Hose: $5\frac{1}{2}$″
Face: Length 2″ Weight 1 lb.
Depth 1″

(c) An iron with a 'cut-off' nose. No maker's name. Certainly a blacksmith-made club probably prior to 1800. A well-lofted club, the face markedly hooked and dished. The hose is large with big knurling. The shaft is of large diameter. There is a thick sheepskin grip.

Length: 35″
Hose: $5\frac{1}{2}$″
Face: Length $3\frac{1}{4}$″ Weight 1 lb.
Depth $1\frac{1}{4}$″

Rutter with 'cut-off' nose

Oval-faced iron, showing hammer marks

(d) An iron with a 'cut-off' nose. No maker's name but a blacksmith-made club certainly before 1820. There is some loft and the face is hooked and dished. There is a large hose with deep, crude, knurling. This club has a curved sole.

Length:	39″	
Hose:	5″	
Face:	Length $3\frac{1}{4}$″	Weight $1\frac{1}{3}$ lb.
	Depth $1\frac{1}{2}$″	

(e) An iron with an oval face. Blacksmith-made and of great age, before 1800. No maker's name. Shaft probably ash. The face is well-hooked and dished and hammer marks can clearly be seen and felt. The hose is crude, large and long.

Length:	37″	
Hose:	6″	
Face:	Length $3\frac{3}{4}$″	Weight $1\frac{1}{2}$ lb.
	Depth $2\frac{1}{2}$″	

(f) Rutting Iron with a 'cut-off' nose. A blacksmith-made club, before 1800. Dished face with some hook. A good stout ash shaft. Undergrip (or rind) only.

Length:	$37\frac{1}{2}$″	
Hose:	4″	
Face:	Length $1\frac{1}{2}$″	Weight 12.5 ozs.
	Depth $1\frac{1}{2}$″	

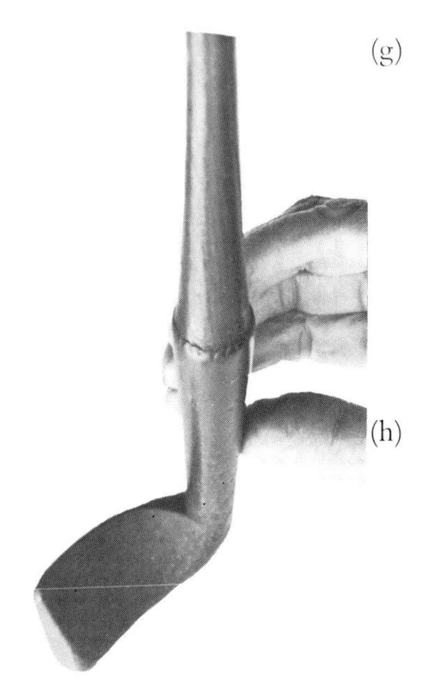

Iron club

(g) Iron putter (probably). No maker's name but the general appearance of the club head suggests a blacksmith-made club of great age, i.e. before 1800. The fact that the shaft appears to be hickory probably means that the club was re-shafted after 1830. The club is of very upright lie. The blade is flat and quite plain and there is no loft. The club could be used either right- or lefthanded.

Length: 31″
Hose: 5″
Face: Length $2\frac{1}{4}$″ Weight 1 lb.
Depth $1\frac{1}{4}$″

(h) Iron with 'cut-off' nose. No maker's name but this is a blacksmith-made club made before 1800. The shaft is very thick and probably ash. The hose is large with crude and deep knurling. The face is well-lofted and markedly hooked and there is a leather grip with a thick underlay.

Length: 35″
Hose: 5″
Face: Length $2\frac{1}{4}$″ Weight $1\frac{1}{3}$ lbs.
Depth 1″

(i) Iron putter. No maker's name. This is almost certainly seen leaning against the wall in the portrait of Mr Henry Callender, Captain of the Blackheath Club, 1797 (see p. 18). A stout ash shaft. The head at 90° to the hose. The blade of the club is plain and there is no loft. The club could be used right- or lefthanded. A very heavy club.

Length: $34\frac{1}{2}$″
Hose: 6″
Face: Length $2\frac{1}{2}$″ Weight $1\frac{3}{4}$ lbs.
Depth $1\frac{1}{2}$″

(j) Giant iron club. No maker's name. This is a very old blacksmith-made club, probably before 1750. A very long, large and heavy club. The face is well lofted, dished and hooked. The hose is massive, the knurling crude and deep. There is a thick underlay but the leather grip is absent. The ash shaft has split under the grip and has been mended.

Length: 47″
Hose: 5″
Face: Length $3\frac{1}{4}$″ Weight $1\frac{3}{4}$ lbs.
Depth $2\frac{1}{2}$″

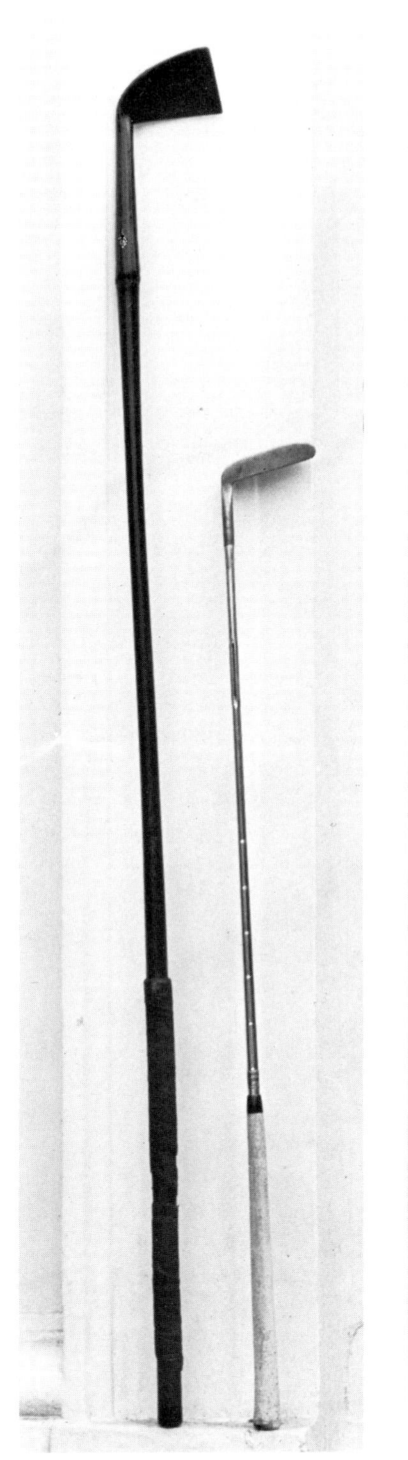

The 'giant' cut-off nose iron; beside it a modern putter, to show the great length of the old club

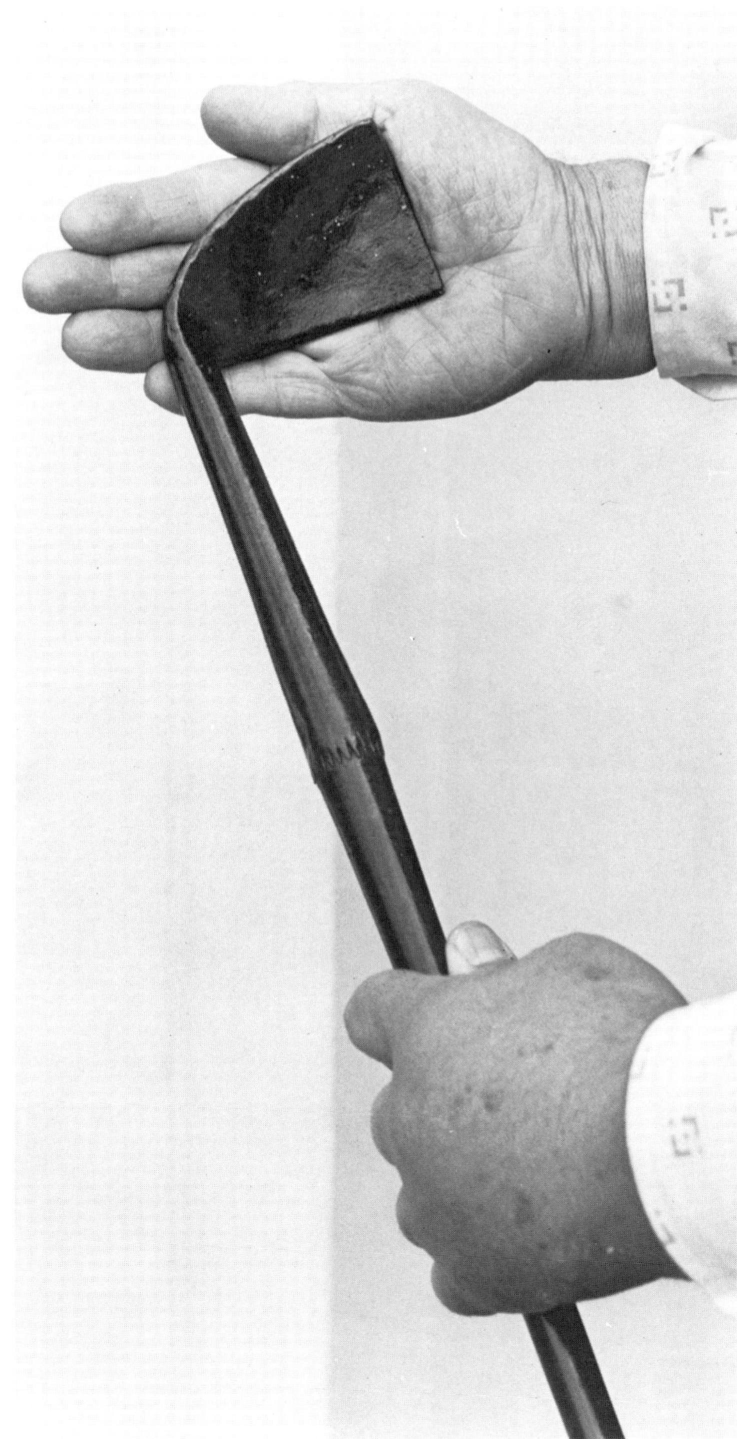

Detail of the head of the 'giant' iron

Chapter 10 Rules of golf at Blackheath

The average Club golfer today is probably no more nor less interested in the Rules of the game than the golfer on Blackheath in 1828–the year in which the Committee of the Blackheath Golf Club revised and amended the 'Laws of Golf', a copy of which is shown on pp. 139–40. The Blackheath golfer of 1828 did however have the advantage, had he decided to study the rules, of finding only nineteen separate Laws or Articles, as compared with the forty-one Rules and three Appendices in the 1980 Code.

The point must be made immediately that the individual Codes of Rules or Laws, laid down or adopted by each Golf Club or Golfing Society, until the latter part of the nineteenth century, were very much in the nature of local rules for Club competitions. Many of the basic rules of the game were unwritten and were part of an oral tradition. It was this tradition to which Captains and Committees had to refer in settling 'ad hoc' disputes referred to them. When in doubt they invoked the spirit of the game. The early Codes which survive–and the 1828 Blackheath Code is no exception–show that the spirit of the game was then considerably sterner than the more equitable spirit which inspires the modern rules.

Just as there was an oral tradition, so were the 'local' rules adapted from one Club to another. The thirteen 'Articles and Laws in playing the Golf' drawn up by the Gentlemen Golfers of Edinburgh in 1744 were the source of the early rules written in St Andrews and elsewhere. All but two of the matters covered by those thirteen Articles are dealt with in the 1828 Blackheath Code but there are significant differences of treatment, for example in the case of 'lost ball' and 'loose impediments' (to use the more modern expression). Though the influence of the Royal & Ancient brought about an increasing standardisation of these local rules–particularly after the coming of the gutta percha ball–local differences continued to exist until the rule-making authority of the Royal & Ancient was finally recognised by all in 1897. A study of the records or the boards displayed in any of the Golf Clubs flourishing in the nineteenth century will disclose how many of the leading golfers of those days were members of more than one Club–even as far apart as St Andrews and Blackheath–and no doubt there were many more who played as visitors on 'foreign' courses. They would, for example, want to know whether a ball lost in the gorse on Blackheath resulted in the hole being lost too, or whether an inadvertent breach of a Rule resulted in loss of hole or a stroke penalty. The latter enquiry would have to be answered at many Clubs by reference to tradition or to the current decisions of the Committee, rather than to the published Codes of Rules, most of which were singularly silent on the subject of penalties.

There is much to interest the student of the game in these local Codes of Rules and it is particularly interesting to note that the Blackheath Committee in 1828 anticipated, by sixty years, the 'lost ball, lost hole' rule of the Royal & Ancient (which operated from 1888 until 1920), and that the present Rule 27–1a and the decisions under it were, in effect, applied by the Blackheath Committee in permitting a ball to be substituted if there was reasonable evidence that the original ball had been carried off by some person or animal. This must have been a common occurrence on Blackheath, where even the flagsticks had to be guarded.

Finally, the Blackheath Committee of 1828 should be praised for the wisdom of their Article XIV which anticipates, almost exactly, the fundamental change in Rule 26–2b of the Rules of Golf made as recently as January 1980.

Blackheath regulations and the Rules of Golf

It has been pointed out that Blackheath had a considerable discipline and administrative ability: this they demonstrated by their strict rules about Club and dinner procedure and by the close attention to their Rules about the actual playing of the game. Nor did they regard the Rules as static but were constantly reviewing and altering them to suit their local conditions. Thus, the first Rules were published in 1828 and there were further Rules published in 1833, 68, 74, 79. In 1889 the Club agreed formally to adopt the Rules of the R. & A. (which by that time were very similar to the Blackheath Rules) saving only the matter of 10 local Rules which were pertinent to their course only. There was one important principle which Blackheath passed on to other English Clubs and which has lead to a difference in development between English and Scottish Clubs. Although Blackheath did not own their course, they saw to it that they, and they alone, had the right to play golf on the Heath. They must have advised other English Clubs to proceed in the same way, for it is a feature of most English Golf Clubs today that they either own it or that their members have the sole right to play on the course.

In Scotland the majority of the courses are publicly owned and several different groups of golfers may play on the same course, which is owned and operated by the local Town Council. This happened at Leith, where there came to be so many golfers that there was no longer room for them and at Musselburgh, where the 9-hole course was owned by Musselburgh Town Council and was used by the Musselburgh Golf Club, the Honourable Company of Edinburgh Golfers, the Edinburgh Burgess Golfing Society and the Bruntsfield Links Golf Club, after the two latter Clubs had had to move from their previous common-ground course near Edinburgh. The Musselburgh Links could also be played on by any ratepayer in Musselburgh. Each Club had its own special tavern or meeting place in the town. The overcrowding here was such that the Honourable Company, the Burgess and Bruntsfield had to move to their own golf courses later. A similar state of affairs still exists at St Andrews where the R & A own their Clubhouse but not their Links, nor do they have the sole right to play on the Links. There are many other examples in Scotland.

Clearly Blackheath, profiting by the experience of their (Scots) members in Scotland, were going to be masters in their own house and were advising the new English Clubs to be sure of their sole right to play on their own course. Blackheath had its own Rules of Golf and freely presented copies to anyone who asked for them (see page 75). Although many of the Rules were local Rules it is a feature of the R. & A., Honourable Company and Blackheath Rules that, in general, they were remarkably similar. This was no accident as the early golfers were a pretty close-knit family. A large number of the early St Andrews golfers came from Edinburgh; the fact that different Golf Clubs used the same course meant that their local Rules would naturally be alike. Blackheath was largely Scot, so they introduced there the Rules that they had learnt in Scotland. After 1864, when Westward Ho! started, to be followed by a large number of Golf Clubs throughout England and Wales, Blackheath members, as has been said earlier, travelled to all these Clubs and played in their meetings so they not only got to know all the local Rules at, say, Westward Ho! Hoylake, Royal Wimbledon and Royal St George's, but probably played a considerable part in helping to formulate them.

The purely local Rules of Golf at Blackheath indicate the particular difficulties of golf on the Heath and the development of some aspects of golf. Such Rules as come to mind are:

1828 XII

A Rule that was particularly apposite on the Heath where dogs, small boys, maliciously inclined, and adults in innocent ignorance (one hopes!) might walk off with a ball.

1879 V

'. . . if the ball lie amongst broken metal, bottles or any substance from which it would be dangerous or objectionable to play, the player may lift the ball . . .' The increasing use of the Heath by the public and the large disused gravel pits must have made a Rule about these sorts of difficulties of particular importance at Blackheath.

1868
'If a ball split or fall to pieces, a fresh ball may be put down near to the largest piece.' This Rule was introduced because of the new gutta ball, which would disintegrate on occasions. Horace Hutchinson remarks in an article on this Rule how frequently the largest piece was to be found on the fairway!

1844
'No party shall drive off until the party in front have played their second shots.' No other course seems to have had this general Rule and today it is a matter of etiquette and not a Rule. It stemmed, probably, from the fact that Blackheath members were very conscious of the possibility of hitting people on the Heath in general, let alone fellow golfers.

1844
'If a ball lie in a supernumerary hole made for the purpose of golfing or any other hole from which it cannot be played or if it be in a cricket tent . . .' Cricket and football were regularly played on the Heath by members of the public.

1891
'. . . a ball lying within two yards of a fixed seat may be dropped two yards to the side of the seat furthest from the hole . . .' Similar rules about lamp posts and ventilation grilles of sewers came at about the same time. They were necessary owing to increasing use of the Heath by the public.

Finally, on 22 March 1904, the Committee considered a new local Rule: 'a ball lodged in the upper part of a lamp post may be removed, or substituted and dropped on the course not nearer the hole, without penalty'. Clearly golf on the Heath had to end! A minute a few weeks after this states that free whisky on Medal Days is to be discontinued, possibly a more depressing Rule than all the others put together. One feature of the Rules of the Game on which Blackheath are to be congratulated is that in 1828 there were only 19 Rules, and these included at least two Rules which are now etiquette rather than Rules. In 1879 there were only 20 Rules–50 years with an increase of one Rule only.

Last, and by no means least, is Rule 16 of 1860 which states, among other things, that each pair is to be accompanied by a marker. It certainly seems to suggest a modicum of distrust about the ability of each of the pair to write the proper score. The full duties of the marker are not stated but, presumably, if he did the job often enough, he must have gained an intimate knowledge of the Rules and, more importantly, have gained a lot of experience in the interpretation of the true spirit of the game. It would have been natural, if a dispute arose between the pair, for them to seek

Caddies retrieving a ball from a lamp post

a solution from a neutral party, just as it would have been natural for him to discuss the decision, after the game, with fellow markers and, perhaps, the Secretary or Captain.

When one considers that scrutineers were appointed at the Dinner, to scrutinise all the cards and see who had won, it must be clear that all the competitors would be satisfied at the end of the day that all was scrupulously fair, honest and above board. This system further demonstrates the ability of Blackheath to ensure a sound administration in all its affairs and possibly the application of this method is one of the reasons why they were able to avoid increasing the number of Rules to try and cover all eventualities, such as is happening at the present time.

'Laws of Golf'

(Revised and amended by the Committee of the BLACKHEATH GOLF CLUB in 1828.)

I 'The distance from the Hole, in Teeing, shall not exceed four club Lengths, nor be nearer it than two, and the Tee must be on the ground.'

II 'The Ball farthest from the Hole played for must be first played.'

III 'Whilst a Stroke is played, none of the Party shall walk about, making any motion, or attempting to take off the Player's attention by speaking or otherwise.'

IV 'The Party gaining a Hole shall strike off first.'

V 'The Ball shall not be changed or handled, on any pretence, whilst playing except when by accident it is driven into water or mud, in which case the Player may take it out, and throw it behind the hazard, losing a stroke.'

VI 'No Stones, Bones, or other Break-clubs shall be removed.'

VII 'If the Player by mistake strikes his Opponent's Ball in playing through the Green, the Stroke shall not be reckoned against either, and the Ball must be played as it may chance to lie.'

VIII 'No person shall be at liberty to better his position in playing, by breaking the surface of the Green, placing or removing stones; but should the Ball be driven into Furze, he shall be at liberty to break down as much of it as will enable him to see the Ball before striking.'

IX 'In playing, no mark shall be used to beat down or make any mark in the sand or soil, whereby to improve the lie of the Ball.'

X 'If a stroke be made, and the Club passes the Ball, or strikes the Ground, it shall be reckoned against the Player, although the Ball be missed, or the Club be broken.'

XI 'The Party whose Ball is amissing shall be allowed five minutes to search for it, after coming to the spot where the Ball appeared to drop. If not then found, the Hole is lost.'

XII 'But should it be evident to both Parties that the Ball must of necessity have been carried off by some person or animal, the loser shall be entitled to throw down another, as near the spot as the Player can guess.'

XIII 'If the Ball be stopped by accident, it must be played as it may chance to lie.'

XIV 'But if stopped by the opposite Party, or their Club-bearers, no stroke shall be reckoned against the Player, and he shall also be at liberty to lay the Ball Fair.'

XV 'At Holing, you are not to mark the direction to the Hole, the Ball must be played honestly for the Hole, and not on the adversary's Ball not lying in the way.'

XVI 'Nothing whatever shall be removed when putting at the Hole, except on the play for the Medal, when all loose impediments, within six club-lengths of the Hole may be removed.'

XVII 'When the Hole is distinctly in view, no person shall stand at it for a direction.'

XVIII 'When several Parties are on the Green, the second Party shall not strike off before each of the advanced Party has played his second Stroke.'

XIX 'If the Player Holes the Opponent's Ball, it shall be reckoned in favour of the Opponent, and be the same as if his Ball had been previously Holed.'

Chapter 11 The ceremony at the Anniversary Dinner and at the 'Wee Dinners'

1 Following the Reception, when Dinner is announced, all go in except the Captain, the Field Marshal, past-Captains and the Captain Elective. They are all in the Club uniform, the Field Marshal with two epaulettes (one on each shoulder), the Captain and Captain Elective with one epaulette on the right shoulder, the past-Captains with none.

2 When all are seated the piper leads the Captain, Field Marshal, past-Captains and Captain Elective around the dining-room, each one dropping off when he reaches his seat.

3 The Captain says Grace.

4 When the Haggis course is reached, the Piper pipes the Haggis around the tables until reaching the Captain, who gives the Piper and the Chef a generous measure of whisky.

5 When the Haggis is served, the Captain initiates the Ceremony of the Quaich. The Captain rises and hands to the member on his left (who also stands) a Quaich and pours whisky into it and bows to that member who also bows to the Captain and immediately turns to the member on his left (who is also standing) bows to him, drinks the whisky and turns over the Quaich to prove it is empty, kisses it and delivers it to the member on his left, and helps him to whisky in the Quaich. This ceremony is repeated round the table, the Captain being the last to empty and kiss the Quaich. (The member receiving and drinking the whisky must always be protected on each side until he has handed over the Quaich.)

6 At the completion of the Dinner, tables are cleared and port circulated. The Captain proposes the loyal toast after which smoking is permitted. There is then a toast to 'Golf and Golfing Societies' and a reply followed by an interval.

7 The Procession. The Secretary then organises the Procession behind the Captain's Chair in the following order: The Piper, Field Marshal (carrying the Field Marshal's Putter), Secretary (Carrying the Ebony Cleek), Senior past-Captain (carrying the Silver Cleek), past-Captains and the Captain Elective. The retiring Captain remains in the Chair. The procession marches clockwise round the table and, on its arrival back at the Captain's

Chair, halts. The Piper ceases playing and steps out of the way. Those in the Procession turn to their right and take up convenient positions. The retiring Captain vacates the Chair. The Secretary replaces the Ebony Cleek, and the Field Marshal's Putter on the Table and takes the Silver Cleek from the Senior past-Captain. The retiring Captain hands the Captain's Badge to the Field Marshal. The Secretary administers the Oath to the Captain Elective, who takes the Oath by kissing the Silver Cleek. The Field Marshal then invests the New Captain with the Captain's Badge. The retiring Captain installs the New Captain in the Captain's Chair. After the New Captain has been installed, the Silver Cleek is replaced on the table and the Procession is dispersed; the Piper plays himself out of the Room.

8 *Captain's Oath* '[Christian names and Surname] you have been elected Captain of this Royal Club by the unanimous vote of its Members. We ask and expect that you will do all that in you lies to maintain its Honour and Dignity, to protect its Privileges and to forward the true interest of Golf. Kiss the Club.'

9 The immediate past-Captain introduces the new Captain and the new Captain replies. The new Captain then asks the Secretary to read out the results of the Autumn Meeting and the New Captain then presents the trophies.

10 There is then a toast to 'The Guests', with reply.

11 'Auld Lang Syne' is sung, standing.

Proceedings at Wee Dinners

When the Club was reorganised in 1843, the dining arrangements were altered and replaced by quarterly dinners which became known as 'The Wee Dinners'. The proceedings of these dinners are as follows:

The Scratch Medal and the Handicap Cup played for on the day of the Wee Dinner are on the dinner table.

When dinner is announced, the Captain accompanied by the Field Marshal and any past-Captains present, precedes the other diners and takes his seat at the head of the table with the Field Marshal on his right. Past-Captains sit on each side of the Captain. Grace is said by the Captain.

After the Haggis the Captain rises and hands to the member on his left (who also stands) a Quaich and pours whisky into it and bows to that member who also bows to the Captain and immediately turns to the member on his left (who is also standing) bows to him, drinks the whisky and turns over the Quaich to prove it is empty, kisses it and delivers it to the member on his left, and helps him to whisky in the Quaich. The ceremony is repeated round the table, the Captain being the last to empty and kiss the Quaich. (The member receiving and drinking the whisky must always be protected on each side until he has handed over the Quaich).

The dinner then proceeds–at its conclusion the Captain gives the toast to the Reigning Monarch and the Loyal Anthem is sung. The Captain then calls upon the Secretary (who usually takes the Vice-Chair) to read out the result of the competitions. The Secretary announces only the Scratch scores–beginnging with the highest scratch return and states the names of the winners, to whom the Captain hands the Medal and Cup respectively with the replicas (if any).

After this, at the Captain's discretion, songs are sung. The cost of the dinner (without wine) is then paid to the Secretary. At the close of dinner, Match Challenges are made; the Captain first calls upon the member on his left hand to make his challenges (which are generally not less than four) and the member pays to the Secretary 25p in respect of each challenge. This proceeds in order round the table, the Captain being the last to make challenges. The amount collected for challenges constitutes a fund for payment for the wine consumed, and is handed to the Secretary for credit to the Wee Dinner Fund. No charge is made at a Wee Dinner in respect of the wine consumed.

A record of Match Challenges made is kept by the Secretary. Each member must make his own arrangements for playing off his dinner matches; if the match is played, and the challenger wins, the loser pays to the challenger the amount of the challenge.

Appendices

List of Scottish Courtiers

James Hamilton, Lord Abercorn
Gentleman of Bedchamber to James VI in 1600. Came to England with him. Was in Ireland from 1613

Sir Robert Kerr (or Carr)
Captain of King's Bodyguard to James VI (resigned in 1613). Created Earl of Ancrum in 1633. Gentleman of Bedchamber to Charles I

John Murray, created *Earl of Annandale* in 1622
Gentleman of Bedchamber and Gentleman of Privy Chamber to James VI and came to England with him in 1603

Sir James Balfour, created *Lord Balfour* in 1619.
Died in London, in 1634

Sir Robert Douglas, created *Viscount of Belhaven* in 1633
Page of Honour and Master of Horse to Henry, Prince of Wales (died 1612). Gentleman of Bedchamber to James VI and to Charles I. Knighted at Whitehall in 1609

Sir James Stewart, Master of Blantyre (son of 1st Lord Blantyre).
Killed in a duel at Islington, 1609, and buried there

Edward Bruce, Lord Bruce of Kinloss
Was Ambassador to England in Queen Elizabeth's reign, and died in London in 1611. His son, Edward Bruce, Lord Kinloss, was a Gentleman of Bedchamber. His brother and heir, Thomas Bruce, was in attendance on James VI for many years. He married in London in 1622 and was created Earl of Elgin in 1633

James Carmichael
Was Cupbearer, Carver and Chamberlain to James I. He was created Lord Carmichael in 1647

John Stewart, Lord Kincleven
Son of the Earl of Orkney, was in London at the start of James I's reign. On October 24, 1604, he was married at Chelsea

James Colville
Was in England in Queen Elizabeth's reign. In 1594 he visited her on an Embassy from Scotland. He was created Lord Colville of Culross in London in 1604

Robert, Lord Crichton of Sanquhar
Married in London in 1608, having been here since at least 1604. He was hanged at Westminster for murder in 1612

Richard Preston
Was a Gentleman of the Bedchamber to James VI and went with him to England in 1603. He attended the Coronation and was created Lord Dingwall in 1609

George Hume, Earl of Dunbar
Was Gentleman of Bedchamber to James VI, and held the life appointment of Master of the Great Wardrobe. He died at Whitehall in 1611

William Murray
Was a boyhood companion of Charles I, and made a Gentleman of the Bedchamber to him in 1626. He was created Earl of Dysart in 1643

Patrick Murray
Studied in England and got his MA in Oxford in 1605. He was admitted to Gray's Inn in 1610. He was created Lord Elibank in 1643

William Hay, Earl of Erroll
Was present at Charles I's Coronation, where he acted as High Constable

Sir John Ramsay, Viscount of Haddington and Lord Ramsay
Was created Earl of Holdernesse in 1621. Dying in 1626, he was buried in Westminster Abbey

James Hamilton, 2nd Marquess of Hamilton
Was Councillor and Gentleman of Bedchamber between 1621 and 1624. He was Lord Steward of the Household in 1624–25. He died at Whitehall in 1625

John Bothwell
Attended James VI and I into England in 1603 as a Privy Councillor of Scotland. He was created Lord Holyroodhouse in 1607

Alexander, Lord Home
Accompanied James VI and I to England in 1603. He became a Privy Councillor of England. He was created Earl of Home in 1604 and died in London in 1619

Thomas Erskine
Was a Gentleman of the Bedchamber from 1585. He attended James VI and I to England in 1603; appointed Captain of the Yeomen of the Guard in that year, and held the appointment until 1617. Created Baron of Dirleton and Erskine in 1604; Viscount of Fentoun, 1606; Earl of Kellie, 1619. Died in London in 1639

George Hay of Kinfauns
Was Gentleman of Privy Chamber from 1612. Created Earl of Kinnoull in 1633. Died in London, 1634

George Hay
Son of the above, known as Viscount Dupplin, was Captain of the Yeoman of the Guard 1632–35

Robert Maclellan
Gentleman of Bedchamber both before and after James VI's accession to the English throne, was created Lord Kirkcudbright in 1633

Ludovic Stuart, Duke of Lennox
Attended James VI and I to England in 1603. Gentleman of Bedchamber and Privy Councillor of England from that year. Died in Holborn in 1623. His brother, Esme, also a Gentleman of Bedchamber, was created Earl of March in 1619. He was made a Knight of the Garter in 1624, the year of his death. Buried in Westminster Abbey

Robert Kerr, Earl of Lothian
Was made KB at the Coronation of James I at Westminster on July 24, 1603. He cut his throat at Newbattle in 1624

John Erskine, Earl of Mar
Followed James VI and I to England in 1603. Although made a Knight of the Garter in that year, he spent most of his life serving James in Scotland

John Erskine, Lord Erskine
Heir of the above, also served the Crown in both England and Scotland

William Keith, Earl Marischal
Lord Keith, was in England in 1625, if not before, and attended the funeral of James I. He was also present at the Coronation of Charles I in *Scotland* in 1633. He had acted as a banker to James I, who borrowed £15,000 from him

William Graham, Earl of Menteith
Was made an English Privy Councillor in 1630. Before that, he seems to have spent most of his time in Scotland, where he was President of the Scottish Privy Council

James Stewart, Earl of Moray
Attended James VI and I to England in 1603, and 'had the entree of the Privy Chamber'. After 1604 he was mostly in Scotland

William Douglas, Earl of Morton
Was Gentleman of Bedchamber from 1613, and a Privy Councillor of England from 1627, having been a member of the Prince's Council from 1624

Alexander Napier
Was a Gentleman of the Privy Chamber to James VI and I whom he accompanied to England in 1603. He mostly served the Crown in Scotland

Robert Maxwell
Created Earl of Nithsdale in 1620, served James VI and I in various ways, in both England and Scotland. He was married in London in 1619

Laurence Oliphant, Lord Oliphant
Was in attendance on James VI and I on his journey to England in 1603

Patrick Maule
Created Earl of Panmure in 1646, had been a boyhood companion to James VI, and accompanied him to England in 1603. He was a Gentleman of the Bedchamber to both James and Charles I. He was appointed Keeper of Eltham Park about 1620

James Drummond, Lord Drummond
Who was created Earl of Perth in 1605, was attached to the English Court. He went on a diplomatic mission to Spain in 1605, and died in 1611

Frederick Stewart, Lord Pittenweem
Was in London in the 1620s and attended the funeral of James VI and I in 1625. It is suggested that he had been in the Fleet Prison. He died in London in 1625 and was buried at St Bride's

Robert Ker
Came to England with James VI and I in 1603 and was created Earl of Roxburghe in 1616. He was made a Gentleman of the Bedchamber in 1607

David Carnegie
Came to England in the train of Anne of Denmark, wife of James VI and I. He was created Lord Carnegie in 1616 and Earl of Southesk in 1633. He served the Crown in many ways, most of them in Scotland

Alexander Lindsay, Lord Spynie
Was in London on and off during the reign of James VI and I, and attended his funeral at Westminster in 1625

William Alexander of Menstrie
Was Gentleman of the Privy Chamber Extraordinary to Prince Henry (d. 1612) from 1607. He was created Viscount Stirling in 1630. He died at his house in Covent Garden in 1640. His son, also William Alexander, was knighted in London in 1626

David Murray
Was a Court servant in Scotland and came to England in 1603 with James VI and I. He was created Lord Scone in 1604. He continued to serve the Crown in Scotland and held many appointments there. He was created Viscount of Stormont in 1621

Trophies and List of Officers

With the exception of the Gold Medal these are on display in the Museum Room, the oldest–the Knuckle Club Medal–having been described already in Chapter 3, p. 27. They are:

A Belonging to the Club before amalgamation with the Eltham Golf Club

Trophy	Year	Details
Spring Medal (Gold) (Originally the Gold Medal of the Knuckle Club)	1789	Stroke
Summer Medal (Gold)	1823	Stroke
Bombay Medal (Silver)	1843	Stroke
Photographic Society's (Gold)	1860	Stroke
George Glennie (Gold)	1881	Stroke
Boys' Medal (Silver)	1847	Scratch. Open to boys who have not reached the age of 17 on the day of the competition and are members of a Golf Club in Kent which is a Member of the Kent County Golf Union.
The above are 'Scratch' medals		
Calcutta Cup	1875	Stroke. Handicaps not over 18
Singapore Cup	1875	Stroke. Handicaps not over 18
Penn Cup	1885	Stroke. Handicaps not over 10. Autumn Meeting. Div. I
Knill Cup	1893	Stroke. Handicaps not over 18
Adam Cup	1897	Stroke. Handicaps not over 18
Queen's Diamond Jubilee Cup	1897	Match Play Singles Tournament
W. G. Kentish Claret Jug	1897	Match Play
	1897	Mixed Foursomes
Great Yarmouth Challenge Bowl	1900	Best aggregate of 2 net scores on any of the 5 Old Royal Blackheath Medal Days. Handicap limited to 18. Ties to be decided under Rules for Stroke Play.
Kennard Jubilee Cup	1903	Full Handicap

B Formerly belonging to the Eltham Golf Club

Trophy	Year	Details
Eltham Scratch Medal (Gold)	1892	Stroke
North Scratch Medal (Gold)	1892	Stroke
Penn Cup	1900	Handicaps 11 to 24. Autumn Meeting. Div. II
Eltham Challenge Cup	1900	Stroke, under handicap

	Swedish Cup	1914 Stroke, under handicap
	Old Blackheathen Vase	1905 Stroke, under handicap
	Royal Artillery Cup	1906 Bogey, under handicap open to Country and Service Members (with a R.B.G.C. Handicap)
	Royal Naval College Challenge Cup	1920 Bogey, under handicap open to Country and Service Members (with a R.B.G.C. Handicap)
C Presented since the amalgamation	Whyte Cup	1925 Bogey, under handicap, open to Country and Service Members (with a R.B.G.C. Handicap)
	Foursomes Challenge Cup	1933 Match play, under handicap
	C. H. Gray Putting Challenge Cup	1932 Open to all Annual Members including Ladies
	J. E. Heath Trophy	1948 Four-ball Bogey to be played for on Spring Bank Holiday
D Belonging to the Ladies' Golf Club before amalgamation with the Eltham Golf Club	Laird Medal (Gold)	1895 Scratch, Bronze Div. Autumn Meeting
	Whyte Medal (Gold)	1898 Scratch, Silver Div. Autumn Meeting
	Spurling Medal (Gold)	1900 Handicap
	Valerie Cup	1890 Scratch. Autumn Meeting
	R.B.G.C. Challenge Vase	1895 Spring Meeting
	Whyte Cup	1897 Medal Winners. Bronze Div.
	Boys' Cup	1899 Scratch. Spring Meeting
	Burman Cup	1910 Best aggregate of 2 net scores. Autumn Meeting.
E Formerly belonging to the Eltham Ladies' Golf Club	Knapping Scratch Medal (Silver)	1896 Autumn Meeting. Bronze Div.
	Eltham Scratch Medal (Gold)	1897 Spring Meeting. Silver Div.
	Diamond Jubilee Cup	1897 Handicap. Spring Meeting
	Whyte Bowl	1903 Medal Winners. Silver Div.
	Latham Cup	1915 Handicap. Autumn Meeting

F Presented for Lady Members since the amalgamation

Ladies' Challenge Cup — 1930 Scratch. Match play
William Gray Challenge Cup — 1931 Match play under handicap

List of Officers

Captain Generals

1801 Henry Callender
1973 G. T. Eagleton

Field Marshals

1802 John Walker
1808 William Wilson
1816 Thomas Longlands
1826 Thomas Jameson
1829 Alexander Innes
1831 George Lindsay
1857 Robert S. Flemyng
1858 Charles Sutherland
1874 Sir Hugh H. Campbell Bt.
1894 Lt. Col. E. H. Kennard
1913 Robert Whyte
1930 Christian H. Gray
1932 J. Steggall Sawyer
1946 W. S. T. Worthington
1956 F. W. Farringdon
1959 W. F. Dyer MC
1965 Cecil W. Leng
1971 Dr J. G. King OBE
1974 Brigadier F. Pocock OBE, MC

Captains

1766 Alexander Duncan
1767 Alexander Duncan
1768 William Wilson
1769 Charles Suttie
1770 Thomas Walker
1771 David Stuart
1772 Charles Suttie
1773 George Alexander
1774 Thomas Walker
1776 Thomas Walker
1777 James Gilmour
1778 William Innes
1781 Thomas Walker
1782 John Walker
1783 Duncan Campbell
1784 Arthur Edie
1785 William Row
1786 Coll Turner
1787 Alexander Learmonth
1788 William Hamilton
1789 Charles Gregorie
1790 Henry Callender
1791 James Duff
1792 Thomas Longlands
1793 George M. Macaulay
1794 Arthur Edie
1795 John Walker
1796 Peter Lawrie
1797 William Christie
1798 Thomas Longlands
1799 Thomas Longlands
1800 John Boyd
1801 Henry Callender
1802 John Walker
1803 Alexander Innes
1804 William Wilson
1805 Thomas Yuill
1806 James B. Duncan
1807 Henry Callender
1808 James Walker
1809 Thomas Longlands
1810 Thomas Jameson
1811 James Loughnan
1812 Gotlieb C. Ruperti
1813 Gotlieb C. Ruperti
1814 William Hood
1815 John Leach
1816 Peter Lawrie
1817 George Lindsay
1818 Charles Laing
1819 Thomas Fennell
1820 George Lindsay
1821 Leslie Finlayson
1822 Leslie Finlayson
1823 Robert S. Flemyng
1824 William A. Cunningham
1825 John Masson
1826 John Robertson
1827 William F. Black
1828 William Black
1829 Archibald Hastie
1830 Alexander Dobie
1831 William Boxill
1832 William Duff
1833 Charles Sutherland
1834 James E. Hadow
1835 Alexander Willis
1836 James Kemp
1837 Capt. P. Cameron
1838 Samuel Granger
1839 Duncan Dunbar
1840 Alexander Hadden
1841 Charles Lewis
1842 George G. Anderson
1843 Alexander Ross
1844 The Hon. Fox Maule
1845 The Hon. Fox Maule
1846 Francis Grant RA
1847 John Hall
1848 Archibald Hastie MP
1849 Archibald Hastie MP
1850 Sir Hugh H. Campbell Bt.
1851 Alexander D. Anderson
1852 Rt. Hon. R. A. Christopher MB
1853 James Campbell
1854 Sir Thomas Moncrieffe Bt.
1856 Archibald Hamilton
1856 Capt. Thomas Crosse
1857 Robert H. Forman
1858 David Henry
1859 Rev. William Marsh
1860 Francis Bennoch
1861 John C. MacDonald
1862 George Glennie
1863 George Glennie
1864 Hayter T. Reed
1865 Samuel W. Hyde
1866 James L. Bennet
1867 James W. Adamson
1868 John A. Rucker
1869 John A. Rucker
1870 Stephen Smith
1871 Henry M. Buskin
1872 William McCandlish
1873 William McCandlish
1874 James L. Bennet
1875 Lt. Col. E. H. Kennard MP
1876 William Kieser
1877 William Kieser
1878 The Hon. Charles Carnegie
1879 Thomas Marsh
1880 Thomas Marsh
1881 John Penn
1882 John Penn
1883 Thomas A. Raynes
1884 Thomas A. Raynes
1885 Frederic Stokes
1886 Frederic Stokes
1887 William G. Barnes
1888 William G. Barnes
1889 Robert Whyte
1890 Robert Whyte
1891 John G. Gibson
1892 John G. Gibson
1893 William E. Hughes
1894 William Morris
1895 Frederick S. Ireland
1896 Frederick S. Ireland
1897 William A. Adam

1898 G. Spurling
1899 H. C. Burton
1900 Dr A. Roper
1901 J. F. Green
1902 A. Spencer
1903 J. L. Low
1904 C. B. Lindsay
1905 G. H. Ireland
1906 E. W. Sampson
1907 J. S. Sawyer
1908 R. Winch
1909 A. C. Latter
1910 C. W. Troughton
1911 W. E. Gray
1912 J. H. W. Davies
1913 C. H. Gray
1914 C. H. Gray
1915 W. E. Gray
1916 W. E. Gray
1917 W. E. Gray
1918 W. E. Gray
1919 P. P. Lincoln
1920 P. P. Lincoln
1921 M. Christopherson
1922 M. Christopherson
1923 C. H. Gray
1924 C. H. Grey
1925 John Eagleton
1926 Col. W. D. Warrington Norris
1927 Col. W. D. Warrington Norris
1928 Maj. Gen. Sir M. Mathew KCMG, CB, DSO
1929 J. E. Heath
1930 F. D. Bartlett
1931 W. D. Willis KC
1932 C. J. T. Robertson OBE, MC
1933 W. Saggers
1934 F. W. Farrington
1935 H. R. J. Rhys
1936 G. T. Eagleton
1937 G. P. Thornton
1938 J. Burrell MC
1939 William F. Dyer MC
1940 William F. Dyer MC
1941 William F. Dyer MC
1942 William F. Dyer MC
1943 William F. Dyer MC
1944 William F. Dyer MC
1945 William F. Dyer MC
1946 J. B. A. Parish
1947 C. W. J. Leng
1948 J. C. Godby
1949 Dr J. G. King OBE
1950 Dr N. M. Ferguson OBE, TD
1951 Brigadier F. Pocock OBE, MC
1952 J. M. Stevenson
1953 A. W. Baker
1954 L. R. Barrett OBE
1955 A. L. Haggerty
1956 A. L. Haggerty
1957 F. M. Passmore MC
1958 C. F. Hopewell
1959 R. G. Hawkins
1960 B. W. Sanderson
1961 F. R. Furber
1962 J. T. Friend
1963 D. W. Walton
1964 E. A. Grafton
1965 F. A. W. Byron CBE
1966 F. J. Bellchambers (died whilst in office)
1966 F. A. W. Byron CBE
1967 N. C. Clark
1968 L. J. Gooch
1969 D. V. H. Edwards
1970 L. W. Wood
1971 H. Lusby BEM
1972 F. D. Tindley DSC
1973 B. S. Mears
1974 R. W. Moore
1975 J. L. Gale
1976 H. J. Cufley
1977 F. C. Bown
1978 H. G. Moxham
1979 D. D. Durban
1980 Cmdr. P. R. G. Worth DSC

Bibliography and Sources of Information

1 The Library of the Royal Blackheath Golf Club–the Minutes Account Books, scrap books, photographic albums etc.

2 The research papers of the Historical Committee of the Royal Blackheath Golf Club.

3 *The Chronicles of Blackheath Golfers* by W. E. Hughes (published privately by Chapman & Hall 1897).

4 *Golf a Royal and Ancient Game* by Robert Clark. 1975 edition, a reprint of the 2nd edition (Macmillan & Co. 1893, first published 1875).

5 *The Story of the R. & A.* by J. B. Salmond (Macmillan & Co. 1956).

6 *A History of Golf* by Robert Browning (J. M. Dent 1955).

7 Unpublished articles by C. B. Clapcott dated May 1939.
'Hon. Company of Edinburgh Golfers on Leith Links 1744–1836',
'On Leith Links 1764–1796',
'Last Days on Leith Links'.

8 *The Chronicles of the Royal Burgess Golfing Society of Edinburgh 1735–1932* by J. Cameron Robbie (Morrison & Cibb Ltd Edinburgh 1936).

9 *St Andrews Home of Golf* by James K. Robertson (J. & G. Innes Ltd Cupar 1976).

10 *The History of the Royal and Ancient Golf Club of St Andrews* by H. S. C. Everard (Blackwood 1897).

11 *The Unlocked Secret* by James Dewar (Kimber 1972).

12 *Illustrations of Masonry* by William Preston (G. Wilkie London 1812).

13 *The Constitution of Free-Masonry* by Lawrence Dermott (T. Burton London 1800).

14 *The Royal Liverpool Golf Club 1869–1932* by Guy B. Farrar (Willmer Brothers & Co. Birkenhead 1933).

15 *Blackheath Centenary 1871–1971* by Neil Rhind (Greater London Council 1971).

16 *Blackheath Village and Environs 1790–1970* by Neil Rhind Bookshop Blackheath Ltd (London 1976).

17 *No. 6 Elliot Place Blackheath. The House and its Occupants 1797–1972* by A. R. Martin FSA.

18 *The Story of the Open Golf Championship 1860–1950* by Charles G. Mortimer and Fred Pignon (Jarrolds Ltd 1952).

19 *Golf in the Making* by Ian T. Henderson and David I. Stirk (Henderson and Stirk Ltd 1979).

Index